# MARRIAGE TO A DIFFICULT MAN
*The "Uncommon Union" of Jonathan and Sarah Edwards*

# MARRIAGE TO A DIFFICULT MAN

*The "Uncommon Union"*
*of Jonathan and Sarah Edwards*

By ELISABETH D. DODDS

THE WESTMINSTER PRESS · Philadelphia

ISBN 0–664–20900–9

LIBRARY OF CONGRESS CATALOG CARD No. 73–141195

PUBLISHED BY THE WESTMINSTER PRESS®
PHILADELPHIA, PENNSYLVANIA

PRINTED IN THE UNITED STATES OF AMERICA

# Contents

# Preface

For ten years I have contended with this material, tried to elude it. Why try to share with our jittery generation a love story from green, smogless colonial New England? What could be more archaic than a report of a faithful marriage and the useful children it produced? But now I feel that there is a point in precisely the anachronism which troubled me: in the contrast between today's casual devaluation of sex and the focused ardor of the Edwardses; between their approach to child-raising and the current skepticism about the family; between today's God, merely one of the milder swearwords, and Edwards' God, the Central Fact. Yes, we are far removed in time and psychological orientation from this pair, but I think their story holds a healing ingredient.

This is no attempt to retread the many biographies of Edwards. Since I am not a professional scholar, that would be impertinent as well as redundant. Instead, I have stressed a side of Edwards that is not generally known. The mythic picture of him is of the stern theologian. He was in fact a tender lover and a father whose children seemed genuinely fond of him.

To probe this marriage, however, is to discover that this was not just a radiant idyll. Here were two exceedingly complex people. An indication of the labyrinthine character of Edwards can be seen in the fact that the major poet, Robert Lowell, tried to write a book about him and quit, defeated by the subject.

To dip beneath the surface saintliness of Edwards' wife is to enter a dark maze of questions. What are the real motivations for self-giving? Is the impulse to sainthood in truth neurotic? At first fascinated by this woman's holiness, I became equally interested that she had not come to it easily. In the middle of her life she briefly entered a period of such confusion that it could be called psychotic. Yet all contemporary reports of her, as well as her mark upon the personalities of her children, indicate that she emerged from this episode with a re-formed personality which survived severe external pressures later. She went on carrying the same heavy load, but carried it as an expression of joy, not of compulsion.

Friends unanimously report that she was one of the rare life-enhancing individuals, ones who make others feel more alive. Moving within the constricting demands of the everyday, she richly responded to the claims of children, friends, tempestuous husband. How did she do it? Or here do we confront the mystery of grace?

A biographer treads a spongy swamp. To tell a straight-forward story full of footnotes leaves unanswered many questions about this intricate relationship. Yet to make a novel of it would be preposterous, an offense to the scrupulously truthful Edwards. How can one stay historically respectable, yet read behind the external evidence? How can one ask whether this woman really adored her husband or whether she was clawed by conflicting feelings about him? Did she welcome all those pregnancies? Is it possible to recapture the real thoughts of remote persons?

All we know about Sarah Edwards is refracted from others. Writing letters was not one of her abilities, and she was too busy to keep a journal. So I have needed occasionally to whittle a new piece to fit a hole in the puzzle. Out of such fragments as we have one can shape a case history, as an anthropologist can take a few fragments of bone and link them upon the armature of his imagination, to reconstruct a creature he has never seen. My product would be, I hope, a parable for the befuddled woman in any period of history. The buried talents, the unfruitful fig tree, the virgins' lamps—these too were parables, out of even remoter time, even stranger cultures. Yet ancient parables can illuminate the contemporary.

A minor explanation. There is an old muddle about the spelling of Sarah's maiden name, Pierrepont. In the Sources is more on this. Here, as in many ways, I defer to Perry Miller, the estimable Edwards scholar. That this project has been finished is testimony to the fortifying patience of David H. Scott. My own family confirm my conviction that home is still where the heart of civilization is, as it was in the eighteenth century.

E.D.D.

# I

## Jonathan Edwards
## Meets His Match

> Some day, after mastering the winds, the waves, the
> tides and gravity, we shall harness—for God—the ener-
> gies of love and then, for the second time in history man
> will have discovered fire.
>
> —*Pierre Teilhard de Chardin*

In 1723 in New Haven, Connecticut, when Yale was a
chaotic young college, an improbable couple met. Shy Jonathan
Edwards was so bright that he had already graduated and
worked nearly a year in New York and was still only twenty
years old. Sarah Pierrepont was a flighty sprite of thirteen. Edwards pursued her solemnly for four years. Then they were
married and their real romance began.

With Sarah, the lonely Edwards was rooted and grounded in
love. She provided him with an orderly routine that hedged
him against distractions and left him free to write his books.
Her character became his proof that the distant God of his
speculations was also a tender personal God who moves about
in the midst of human affairs. In the last moment of Edwards'
life he did not speak about theology. He spoke of Sarah and
their "uncommon union."

But it is remarkable that these two survived their courtship.
Moody, socially bumbling, barricaded behind the stateliness of
the very shy, Edwards was totally unlike the girl who fatefully
caught his eye. She was a vibrant brunette, with erect posture

and burnished manners. She was skillful at small talk—he had no talent for it at all. She was blithe—he given to black patches of introspection.

Yale was full of other young men who could crack a casual joke or swoop up gracefully on ice skates to invite Sarah to glide around a pond with them. (Edwards was the kind of gawky boy whose ankles would have wobbled.) When he first showed an interest in Sarah, he scared her.

Already it was clear that this glowering young man was touched by the fatal ingredient of greatness. Though one of the youngest members of his class—he had entered college at the age of thirteen—he had been the valedictory orator in 1720. Back now to work as a tutor and pursue a graduate degree, he was collecting a reputation as a formidable intellect.

Physically, too, he was marked by an odd sort of majesty. Men in the eighteenth century were short, but Edwards, six feet and then some, towered over his contemporaries. He had "unusually piercing, luminous eyes." Even his eating habits made him different from other people. That was an era of jolly gorging. Fish, game, and poultry abounded. Gingerbread, hot muffins, jam, home-produced honey, covered every table, but Edwards picked at a plate and admonished himself in his journal in September, 1723: "By sparingness in diet and eating as much as may be what is light and easy of digestion, I shall doubtless be able to think more clearly and shall gain time 1. by lengthening out my life; 2. shall need less time for digestion after meals; 3. shall be able to study more closely." Edwards also was different because he was not a drinker. Puritans consumed hard liquor in astonishing quantities. Edwards' own father turned out a locally famed hard cider in the orchard behind his house. One Massachusetts town of forty families managed in 1721 to tuck away three thousand barrels of hard cider. But Edwards would lurk in a corner for a whole evening, fiddling with a single glass while the punch bowl emptied and refilled and other young men around him grew flushed, slapped backs, told gamy jokes. Few people knew Edwards well enough to jab him genially in the ribs. Often people who turn out to be the most interesting adults are the ones least acceptable to their adolescent peers. This is painful at the age when popularity is the measure of a person's sense of self-worth. The greatest discomfort for an adolescent is to jut out from a crowd, and Edwards was painfully conspicuous.

At first when Edwards lingered at the doorstep of the church, hoping to speak to the preacher's daughter, he did not realize she was trying to avoid him, for Sarah had been exquisitely trained in courtesy. She had been raised a Pierrepont. Today, status is slippery and many scramble for it, but the Pierreponts never thought about status. That they were serenely supreme is indicated by the ranking of Sarah's brother in his Yale class. Midway in the freshman year the names of the newest class were posted in the buttery (snack bar). The list ranked boys by social standing and a boy was stuck with that rating for four years. Harvard had the same cruel custom, but there the rating was half on the basis of academic promise. At Yale, where the rating was entirely social, Sarah's brother led his list.

Their father, James Pierrepont, was for thirty years minister of the church in New Haven, at a time when clergy dominated the political life of the colonies. James Pierrepont is said to have made the motion that Yale be founded, and his was the leading voice in the Saybrook Synod, a gathering in 1708 which fixed church polity—and hence the political and social order—of New England for half a century.

Pierrepont was a Harvard graduate who had married the granddaughter of John Davenport, a forceful man who was New Haven's first minister. She caught a fatal cold early in her marriage, and Pierrepont's second wife also lived only a short time. Then he made a brilliant third marriage to Mary Hooker, who was to be the mother of Sarah.

Mary came of even more lustrous lineage than James did. One of her grandfathers was Thomas Willet, first mayor of New York City. Her other grandfather was Thomas Hooker, a personality so commanding that even Cotton Mather said of

him that he "could put a king in his pocket." In 1636, Hooker
had found the Massachusetts Bay Colony cramped. He said it
was "like a hive overcrowded with bees," so he led his Cambridge congregation away. They followed Indian trails to a
fertile bend in the Connecticut River at the place where Hartford, Connecticut, now stands.

There these jaunty settlers organized two towns, chose delegates to a General Court, and drew up a set of laws that they
managed to avoid sending back to England for approval by the
king as other colonies had to do. Under Hooker's exhilarating
leadership, the state of Connecticut began in a mood of confidence. It was the first sign of the independence that led to
the Revolutionary War.

Thomas Hooker's traits of charm, practicality, and tact all
reappeared in his great-granddaughter Sarah. She was raised in
a house that had been built for her father by his congregation
in 1686 on the corner of Elm and Temple Streets. It was the
first of a line of dwellings that New Haveners came to call
"Quality Row." These houses, enclosing a common green where
cattle grazed, were of a straightforward design, shaped in part
by the demands of harsh weather, in part by the taste of carpenters and the materials available to them. These men built
supremely well, both from internal standards of workmanship
and also because everyone in town knew who had worked on
what job. As a result, the artless carpenters of colonial New
England produced an architecture of restrained elegance and
unmatched pleasantness.

While they were building Sarah's house, one of the parishioners, a modest farmer named William Cooper, wanted to
make a contribution. He had little else to donate, so he dug up
two elm saplings and installed the tiny trees on the lawn of
the new house. Some other church members thought the trees
should have been mulberry so the minister could raise his own
silkworms. (Their reaction is yet another evidence that whatever is done in any church will be disapproved by someone.)
But the trees thrived and were the first of the noble elms for

which New Haven calls itself "The Elm City."

While Sarah was growing up, New Haven was a pretty town, with four public buildings—a meetinghouse, a jail, a guard-house, a grammar school—all clustered about a common pasture. Its busy harbor was so shallow that ships rested on the bottom at low tide. In order to lure an iron foundry to the village and save the cost of importing tools, the townspeople had donated 140 days of free labor to build the foundry, and stockholders were spared taxes on their investment in it. The town bustled with prosperity. There was no further need to be alert for Indian raids, and the grinding work of clearing stumps and rocks from fields was over. Each house had a garden and in the evening the cows came home from the common pasture to be milked in their own barns. It was a period of repose after toil and danger—one Puritan preacher described it as "a summer season." So it was a happy time to be young, and Sarah's family had given her a comfortable childhood.

In addition to his salary, James Pierrepont had income from land and from inheritances. When the outlying common fields around New Haven had been distributed among the townspeople, Pierrepont acquired a salt marsh, as well as 150 acres "upland East side of East River near Mr. Yale's farm also 12 acres bog meadow adjoining." So there was a margin of money for extra comforts in the Pierrepont house. James even had a luxury few ministers have today—two new silk-crepe pulpit gowns in one six years' period.

Though Puritans looked dourly upon the education of women, whose minds were reputedly weaker than a man's, Sarah had the best training a girl was allowed to have then. In 1711, James ordered a hornbook, a small board with a handle which a child could hold while reading the Lord's Prayer on one side, on the other, the alphabet. But Sarah's education and that of Jonathan's sisters went considerably beyond this crude tool. These girls came from exceptional families and they were tutored at home by ambitious, cultivated parents. However, Sarah always was a shaky speller. This, and a vagueness about

arithmetic, seems to have been a characteristic of even privileged girls then. A New Haven girl of similar background had
such difficulties that after she had been married ten years her
brother was still twitting her: "I suppose sister is still learning
the Mutiplication Table. I would not have her discouraged,
she will get through it by the time she is 50 or 60."

Of course Sarah learned to sew, knit, do patchwork, and
recite the Catechism. Young ladies of quality were also expected to play a musical instrument. Sarah learned the lute,
and later Edwards was often to tuck into his pocket a reminder
to buy a new lute string on his travels. No girl in those days
was allowed to slouch. She was made to practice good posture
by walking with a book on her head for many tedious hours. By
the time Sarah became the uneasy object of Edward's awkward advances she stood instinctively with lifted chin.

Though only one portrait of her remains, Sarah is mirrored
clearly in the reports of people who met her. Some persons
leave contradictory impressions, so the comments about them
vary. The observations of those who knew Sarah Pierrepont
have complete consistency. Everyone mentions her beauty and
her way of putting people at ease. Samuel Hopkins, a friend
who has left the earliest memoir of the Edwards family, stressed
her "peculiar loveliness of expression, the combined result of
goodness and intelligence." Once Edwards saw her, he was
stunned.

He took to walking past her house at night for a glimpse of
a candle flickering behind an upstairs shutter. When a boat
came into Long Wharf with a cargo from England, he would
manage to be around as it was unloaded. Almost every ship
from England brought a box for the Pierreponts, and there was
a chance that James would bring a daughter down with him
as he checked his orders for mace, allspice, white sugar, saffron,
and mirrors for the ladies of his household. Edwards even tried
to improve his social dexterity, and admonished himself, "Have
lately erred, in not allowing time enough for conversation."

At the close of the school term, he went home to East

Windsor, Connecticut, a town that had originally been named Podunk, the Indian word for "cornfield." There he was supposed to prepare for his M.A. degree. He had work to do, for he had to write an original paper on logic, natural philosophy, or metaphysics, and also to compose some theory in theology that he was scheduled to defend in debate with the faculty. Edwards was a compulsive student, but he paced the room, sharpened his quill pen and then resharpened it, gazed out of the window, and finally in the front page of a Greek grammar book, he wrote this famous description:

> They say there is a young lady in [New Haven] who is beloved of that Great Being, who made and rules the world, and that there are certain seasons in which this Great Being, in some way or another invisible, comes to her and fills her mind with exceeding sweet delight, and that she hardly cares for anything except to meditate on him. . . .
>
> Therefore, if you present all the world before her, with the richest of its treasures, she disregards it and cares not for it, and is unmindful of any pain or affliction. She has a strange sweetness in her mind, and singular purity in her affections; is most just and conscientious in all her conduct; and you could not persuade her to do anything wrong or sinful if you would give her all the world. . . . She is of a wonderful sweetness, calmness and universal benevolence of mind. . . .
>
> She will sometimes go about from place to place, singing sweetly and seems to be always full of joy and pleasure; and no one knows for what. She loves to be alone, walking in the fields and groves, and seems to have someone invisible always conversing with her.

But the object of this digression from Greek grammar sensed that life with a man like Edwards would be larger than life-size. There were other men about, of sunnier temperament and blander talents. So Sarah gave Edwards three hard years.

# II

## A Checkered Courtship

The man whose heart is endeared to the woman he loves, he dreams of her in the night, hath her in his eye and apprehension when he awakes, museth on her as he sits at table.

*—Thomas Hooker*

Some qualities that make an admirable husband make a dismal beau. Edwards' massive loyalty was a sterling attribute in a spouse, but it made him a trying swain. It was characteristic of him to pick out one girl to adore, for he hadn't the talent for skating over the surface of many casual relationships, flirting with many girls. So he would watch Sarah with a circle of young people and then when he finally had a chance to talk to her, he would be gruff. Back in his room, he would confide to his journal: "A virtue which I need in a higher degree . . . is gentleness. If I had more of an air of gentleness, I should be much mended."

At home in East Windsor, he had been accustomed to coddling from women, for he was an only son with ten sisters. The girls were all so tall that Timothy Edwards, their father, referred jocularly to his "sixty feet of daughters." Timothy, a graduate of Harvard, and the son of a prosperous merchant, had come to Connecticut in 1694. His wife was the daughter of Solomon Stoddard, the most powerful figure in the Connecticut River Valley. The Indians found Stoddard so imposing that they called him "the White Man's God," though he was, as a matter of fact, merely a clergyman. Esther Stoddard Edwards was a strong personality herself. She was highly intelligent and so robust that when she reached her nineties, she was still holding afternoon salons for the discussion of books. The forceful mother and ten sisters had accustomed Edwards to the admiring attention of women. Sarah was something strange for him to absorb.

Edwards had achieved a degree of self-confidence during the successful period he had just spent in New York City, serving a small Presbyterian church in a cluster of Dutch-style houses around a breezy harbor. He worked competently there and made friends whom he kept for life. After that year he wavered between an offer from a parish in Bolton, Connecticut, and the option of returning to Yale for his advanced degree. By choosing New Haven, he stepped into a chaotic situation.

In 1722, Timothy Cutler, rector (president) of the college, had showed a leaning toward Episcopalianism. This seemed a shocking aberration to Puritans whose parents had left their home country to escape the domination of the Church of England. A stormy scene between Cutler and the trustees ended with the dismissal of the rector and three tutors who supported him. Cutler went to England and confirmed the apprehension of the trustees by actually changing over to become an Episcopalian. Edwards was rocked. He had considered Cutler both a friend and sponsor. When the rector first met Jonathan in 1719 he had written to Timothy Edwards: "I congratulate you upon his promising abilities and advances in learning. He is now under my care and probably may continue so."

The Cutler affair demoralized Yale as well as Edwards. In the year that followed, almost the whole responsibility for holding the college together crashed down on three remaining tutors. Even under easy circumstances, a tutor had a rigorous role. He had not only to maintain order among the rambunctious students in the dormitories but to drill them in their lessons and organize the debates that were held twice a week in the dining hall. A tutor was in a tricky role as a disciplinarian, for he was paid only a pittance and counted on gifts from students to supplement his income. Students everywhere were feeling frisky in that period after the first years of austerity in Puritan society. Bundling and dancing were common and even ordinations were alcoholic events. There is recorded in "The Acts and Judgements of the President and Tutors at Yale College" the story of one evening during which undergraduates stamped and jumped until they broke the plaster and when the tutors sent for them, they "behaved with the utmost insolence, Contempt and Disrespect." To rein in such jovial commotion was hard employment for a man like Edwards, but he reminded himself to "keep a benign aspect and air of acting and speaking in all places and in all companies, except it should so happen that duty requires otherwise."

Edwards wrote this in the journal he intermittently kept from December, 1722, until June, 1726, the years of his courtship. It gives us a picture of the miseries of a genius in love. He intended the diary to be destroyed at his death, but it was not with him when he died. To keep the record private, he wrote delicate passages in a shorthand he had invented. His handwriting discourages the snooper, for it was a tiny scrawl, aggravated by his habit of saving paper by writing up and down across lines.

His handwriting shows the strain he was undergoing. In the first pages it was small but neat. By 1725, his most agitated year, it became spiky and taut and the entries went like these:

| December 29 | Dull and lifeless |
| January 9 | Decayed |
| January 10 | Recovering |

Lonely on the social periphery, pressured in his job, insecure in his courtship, Edwards had sunk into the period of floundering that often characterizes the spiritual pilgrimage of an unusual man. At the same time in England ugly, depressed Samuel Johnson had dropped out of Oxford. There is a long list of young men who threshed about uncomfortably before they were able to come to terms with the extraordinary personalities they had been given.

The consciousness of sin that weighed on every serious Puritan was exacerbated in Edwards by his powerful emotions about Sarah. He once sternly instructed himself to think of a safe subject such as arithmetic: "When I am violently beset with temptation or cannot rid myself of evil thoughts, to do some sum in arithmetic or geometry or some other study, which necessarily engages all my thoughts and unavoidably keeps them from wandering."

The Yale trustees had noted how hard Edwards was working to help hold the college together, and at the commencement in 1725 he got a raise. "The Tutors for their extraordinary Services of the year past and their trouble and pains in sorting the books and fixing Catalogues to ye Boxes have five pounds each added to their salary." A subsequent history of Yale acknowledged: "The Hon. Wm. Smith, the Hon. Daniel Edwards [an uncle of Jonathan's] and the Rev. President Edwards were the pillar tutors and the glory of the college at the critical period. . . . Almost the entire government and instruction of the college fell upon these men."

Then physical illness provided Edwards with the complete change of pace he needed. When he started riding home after the commencement, he was feeling dreadful. Each mile he felt worse and he made it only as far as North Haven, where he collapsed with pleurisy at the house of his friend, Isaac Stiles, who had just moved there with his bride. He was ill so long that his mother came down to nurse him. The Stiles and Edwards families intertwined for several generations. Isaac Stiles had been a weaver in East Windsor when Timothy Edwards persuaded him to get an education, so he went to Yale when he was twenty years old. As a result of this decision to switch careers, Isaac's family produced a president of Yale (from 1777 to 1795) in Ezra Stiles. Timothy Edwards worried about the bother his sick son had caused the newlywed Isaac

Stiles, and wrote his own wife, "Forget not to thank Mr. Stiles and Mistress for any kindness they have showed you," and then he added an admonition typical of a fussy father: "Put Jon. in mind to pay Mr. Stiles."

From this low point, Edwards mended. The desperate interval had been for him like the experience a beginner has in learning to make pottery. He fights the clay, pushing with all his strength against the whirling blob on the wheel, but it seems to have a wicked will of its own, resisting the hand of the clumsy potter. Then comes the moment when the clay is mysteriously "centered." It touches the spot where it should be and settles, peaceful and pliant. At last the process of shaping can begin.

Edwards finally knew what kind of man he had to be and from then on he was integrated, the parts of him staying together under stress. He had centered down. His diary after his return to New Haven for the new school year shows signs of vitality surging back. He wins the affection of the reader with this comment: "It is better that the prayer be of almost any shortness than that my mind should be almost continually off what I say." He began to try harder in the social graces, and reminded himself: "One thing wherein I have erred, as I would be complete in all social duties, is in neglecting to write letters to friends."

He was less prickly, so the courtship began to run more smoothly. Both Edwards and Sarah enjoyed tramping on beaches and through woods. Sarah discovered that the young man who had at first appeared pallidly bookish was an observant naturalist and a stimulating guide to nature. At the age of twelve he had written an essay on the habits of insects and another remarkable study about rainbows. He records this healthy, entirely human response to one day of wonderful weather: "Sometimes on fair days I find myself more particularly disposed to regard the glories of the world than to betake myself to the study of serious religion."

Sarah shared Edwards' sensitivity to the beauty of their surroundings. In those days, New Haven, which was contained between two high rock formations and faced the endless variety of the sea, was a fortunate setting for two confirmed walkers. When winter turned life inward, there beauty surrounded them too. New Englanders had learned early how to wrap coziness around them against the outdoor chill. In the handsome Pierrepont house, fireplaces in each room not only held off cold but provided glowing centers of light that glinted on brightly polished brass andirons and cherrywood tables. Snug inside when November sleet fell, Jonathan and Sarah discovered that they could talk comfortably about books together. Sarah introduced Edwards to her own copy of a book by Peter Maastricht which was to influence Edwards' thought about the nature of the Covenant. Edwards' enthusiasm about the Yale Library made Sarah's father purr, for that was a project close to the heart of James Pierrepont.

Soon after Pierrepont had supervised the transfer of some church land for the first college building, he gathered ten clergymen around a table in a neighboring parsonage. Pierrepont put six of his own books on the table and said, "I give these books for the founding of a college in this colony." The other men added some books from their own shelves, and forty-one books collected that day started the Yale Library. Then in 1712, Pierrepont, through the agent for Connecticut Colony in England, reached the ear and pocketbook of Elihu Yale. From this governor of the East India Company, the new college received a donation of books by secular authors—Locke, Newton, Defoe, Addison, Steele. One of the most ardent users of the new books was Edwards. James Pierrepont liked that.

He also had kept an eye on the way the young man had helped steer the new school through its precarious year. This young man, James and Mary Pierrepont concluded, had a promising future.

Edwards was finally ready to accept himself, so Sarah accepted him. His feelings about the engagement are revealed in a letter he wrote to her, pressing for her to set an early marriage date. "Patience," he wrote, "is commonly esteemed a virtue but in this case I may almost regard it as a vice." Sarah was seventeen, Edwards twenty-four.

It was customary for girls then to marry before they were sixteen. This was realistic in view of the slim life expectancy in those days—about thirty-three years. But Sarah had dawdled about taking the step. Even before she had had a husband in mind, though, she had, like all aristocratic young girls then, spent many hours spinning linen, stitching, hemming. One item on which a girl always worked for her hope chest was a huge pile of napkins—a necessity in those days of few forks. The *New England Weekly Journal* in 1733 announced that "no maiden properly brought up would think herself prepared to marry until she had at least 10 pr. linen sheets." Sarah, stitching away quietly, had many hours to think about the large commitment she was making, for Puritans took marriage very seriously. Wives were well protected by law, and a man could be punished for using "harsh words" to his wife, while a woman was fined for a "shrewish tongue." The stability of a family was immensely important to the continuity of the new society that had ventured so far across so perilous an ocean.

The Puritan view of marriage was not the bloodless one we now mistakenly associate with the word "Puritan." Alienation from the body was a Victorian aberration. The real Puritans loved well and were not ashamed to enjoy it. Sarah's wedding dress expressed the mood. No white wraith mistily drifting toward some vague spiritual experience, she wore a pea-green satin brocade with a bold pattern as she stepped joyfully toward her lover. (During the days of Martha Washington a misguided descendant remodeled that dress in a style which copied the First Lady's fashions.) Edwards met her on July 28, 1727, wearing a new powdered wig and a new set of white clerical bands given to him by his sister Mary, his closest friend in the family.

No purple diary remains to make their passion explicit, but there is external evidence of harmony and relaxation. In Sarah the lonely spirit of Edwards found its sunlit harbor. The emotional center of this many-layered marriage we can no more surmise than we can say for sure what went on in the mind of Mozart. The inner truth about Jonathan and Sarah Edwards was locked between them.

How Edwards felt about it shows in reflected glints. He preached meltingly on Gen. 2:21–25, the story of how "when Adam rose from his deep sleep God brought woman to him from near his heart." And in his notebook he wrote: "When we have the idea of another's love to a thing, if it be the love of a man to a woman . . . we have not generally any further idea at all of his love, we only have an idea of his actions that are the effects of love. . . . We have a faint, vanishing notion of their affections."

# III

## "Yes, Yours, My Love, Is the Right Human Face"

And no person of discernment could be conversant in the family without observing and admiring the perfect harmony and mutual love and esteem that subsisted between them.

—*Samuel Hopkins*

They traveled together to their first home along what John Adams called "the finest ride in America." The Connecticut was then a shining river, and on it sloops winged from Saybrook on the Sound to Hartford, carrying sugar, rum, molasses, and iron. A trail worn smooth and wide enough for oxcarts followed the water. Just beyond Wethersfield, famous for its onion beds and pretty girls, the newlyweds came to the lively port of Hartford, where vessels sometimes lined up three-deep at the wharves. Nearby, in East Windsor, Edwards' parents provided a comfortable stopping place.

Beyond Hartford the river was too tricky for sloops, so traffic was transferred to clumsy flatboats poled by husky men. At Longmeadow the river was its widest—2,100 feet between its banks—then it closed upon a gorge and a falls at South Hadley. Now the smell of wilderness was on the left of the horseback rider, coming from tangles of wild grapes, raspberries, plums, bayberries, and currants on hills where panthers, lynx, bobcat, and bear still padded through the woods.

At Mt. Tom and Mt. Holyoke, the river opened again on a

wide panorama of incomparable scenery as far as the border of
Vermont. Soon the Edwardses saw a line of canoes tied to stakes
along the shore. (Farmers fastened their craft so they could
paddle out to fish or to reach their outlying "lotts".) It is
probable that the young Edwardses had picked up horses at
East Windsor, after leaving the boat at Hartford. In any event,
they followed the river. Then, where a small stream slipped
down from gentle hills, they turned inland, as had the settlers
from Hartford who had in 1654 scuffled through underbrush
to reach a site they named Northampton. By 1655 this group
had built a sawmill, gristmill, and a square meetinghouse with
a thatched roof. Each new township, in order to qualify for
charter, had to "settle a learned, orthodox minister," clear five
acres of grass, and stake out sixty-three lots, allowing two for
ministers and one for a school. The first twenty-five settlers
from Hartford had met all these requirements and still had so
much energy left to produce offspring that by 1661 they had
already outgrown their first meetinghouse.

They turned the first church building into a school and built
a grander one with a high turreted roof. Jedediah Strong was
hired in 1677 to blow a conch shell to summon congregations
to the compulsory services. That same year the building had
been fortified against Indians, as a result of some unpleasantness at nearby Hatfield. A frontier mood still lingered in that
area of mountainous western Massachusetts when the Edwardses first arrived in the settlement. At Northfield, on its
breathtaking site up the river a bit, was a fort. Only a few
canoes carrying trappers and soldiers had ventured much beyond. However, Northampton land was becoming valuable. At
Pocumtuck, a twenty-five-mile tract north of town had been
divided into "cow commons, sheep and goat commons" and
traded on the Boston market as stocks might be today. There
were six hundred parishioners living in the town when a tired
Sarah stepped down from her horse and, stretching legs limp
from the long ride, looked around at her new home.

At first the couple stayed with Jonathan's grandfather, Solo-

mon Stoddard. One indication of the force of Stoddard's character was the width of the road between Northampton and
Boston. Stoddard liked to attend Harvard commencements,
but he preferred to go in a wheeled vehicle. So he had
badgered the Commonwealth of Massachusetts to widen the
horseback trail.

Stoddard hadn't missed a preaching appointment in fifty-
nine years, and after so many years of being heard with respect
he spoke as if each word he dropped was a golden globule.
Secure in honors, snug in a house of an elegance surprising for
a region on the frontier, Stoddard was now eighty-five and
ready to take it easier. His grandson was supposed to free Stoddard from preaching every other Sunday, and it was understood
that Edwards would inherit the pulpit. This was an impossible
expectation. A young man was asked to fill the place of a
predecessor who was inimitable.

Any beautiful newcomer in a small town was a curio, but
when she was also the wife of the new minister, she caused
intense interest. The rigid seating charts of churches at that
time marked a minister's family as effectively as if a flag flew
over the pew. All women were conscious of scrutiny on Sunday. (The dressmaker for one Waterbury, Connecticut, family
used to ask before she designed a hat for a woman, "Which
side is your meetinghouse side?") During the week frontier
women trudged between well, woodpile, and clothesline, but
on Sunday they had a chance to see their neighbors, catch up
on the news, expand their little worlds of housekeeping. So
every eye in town was on Sarah as she swished in wearing her
wedding dress.

Custom commanded that a bride on her first Sunday in
church wear her wedding dress and turn slowly so everyone
could have a good look at it. Brides also had the privilege of
choosing the text for the first Sunday after their wedding. There
is no record of the text Sarah chose, but her favorite verse was
"Who shall separate us from the love of Christ?" (Rom. 8:35),
and it is possible that she chose to hear that one expounded.

She took her place in the seat that was to symbolize her role
—a high bench facing the congregation, where everyone could
notice the least flicker of expression. Sarah had been prepared
for this exposed position every Sunday of her childhood on the
leafy common of New Haven, but it was different to be, herself, the Minister's Wife. Other women could yawn or furtively
twitch a numbed foot in the cold of a January morning in an
unheated building. Never she. Others could have weekday
lapses—snarl at stupid tradesmen or admit to simple fatigue—
but when the minister's wife showed human frailties, it was
the subject of conversation.

During the morning worship the man in the pulpit was a
stranger to her. He who had a few hours before been a bony
boy in her bed was now lifted into majesty by his mighty sense
of his calling. The pulpit in colonial buildings was no architectural caprice—it was elevated to symbolize the vocation that
lifts a man. Anyone who climbs those steps becomes the
spokesman for the Living God. Edwards believed completely
that each Sunday he broke open the Word of God himself,
so for him each Sunday was an awesome encounter. He never
gave a hint of recognition when he caught Sarah's eye. Instead,
he stared over the heads of the congregation at the bellpull
that hung against the rear wall. Sarah's turn came later. At
noon she could offer him a warm room, a meal tailored to his
fluttery digestion, a few hours' respite before the afternoon
service. He might even indulge in the earthy pleasure of a nap.

From that first Sunday, Sarah encountered a factor that was
to color the Edwardses' relationship to each other. Even in
those days the majority of church members in New England
were women. (The ratio varied between two to one and three
to one, depending on the year and the town.) Sarah had to
learn to live with the fact that her husband was the central male
figure for many solitary women. Single aunts had no option
except to live in the houses of relatives—helping to can cherries
from another woman's orchard, taking care of another woman's
babies—or they drudged along caring for aging parents or were

lone widows. Their emotional needs were great, and in those
lean lives the minister was one figure of masculine importance.
So from the start Sarah had to share her husband not only
with the claims of his duty to God's will but with the tugs of
parishioners.

Though the bride and groom were bundled in comfort at
the Stoddard house, with servants to see that a copper warming
pan waited in their bed on chilly nights and that hot muffins
were ready for breakfast, the Edwardses were eager to be in
their own house. They had a site on a place where an earlier
house had been burned by Indians, so it was not like hacking
out untouched soil. The land had the look of earth that had
been already trampled by feet, warmed by fire, turned by a hoe.
As a stair rail is smoothed by hands sliding along its surface,
so a used piece of land has the marks of life—a clump of
peonies, a lilac bush, a path to a privy, a worn place by the
kitchen door where clothes were hung out to dry.

On this plot the Edwardses built a simple, foursquare house
in a quarter acre of garden, bounded by a slab fence. Only five
Northampton houses were painted at that time, but probably
the Edwards dwelling was one of the five. The chaste white
buildings of the New England cliché did not appear until later,
so the Edwardses' new clapboard house was perhaps a jaunty
red or green, with black shutters. It had a small front hall,
enhanced by a handsome walnut drop-leaf table with beauti-
fully burnished finish, which can still be seen today in the
house of a Princeton dean. A stairway rose steeply, outlined by
a mahogany railing. (A piece of that wood is preserved in a
gavel at Princeton.) The light that filtered in was almost sub-
marine, coming through uneven glass windows. Glass was crude,
scarce, and costly, for it had to be brought from England. No
glass factories succeeded in America until 1737. There were
no window blinds—only heavy indoor shutters, a relic of the
days of Indian arrows. The absence of blinds meant lack of
privacy. Fascinated speculation was stirred if the windows were
shuttered for any reason but a storm. So passersby all gazed

at Sarah's wedding gifts: a mirror with an elaborate frame; a Windsor chair, which was a novelty in that period of banister-back chairs; a silver saltcellar; a stunning squat silver porringer that had belonged to the Stoddards. Many people then ate from wooden trenchers, but the Edwardses ate from pewter dishes. The interior of their house was most of all distinctive because it was full of books.

Actually the Edwardses lived frugally, but it was instinctive with Sarah to do ordinary tasks with flair. She was the kind of woman who took the trouble to tie her hair with a ribbon for breakfast when many wives came down tousled; who spent an extra minute to stamp a design on a block of home-churned butter; who knew how to give a flourish to simple dishes with parsley, spearmint, or sage, all grown in a square of herbs by the kitchen door; who, when she had a bowl of peas to shell, would take it out into the sunshine in the garden. She put in day lilies, hollyhocks, pansies, pinks—the flowers women loved to plant on the frontier, for it gave them a sense of putting down roots. Wallpaper wasn't used until 1740 in the colonies, but New Haven had been one of the first towns to use plaster on interiors, so it is possible that Sarah had brought up with her the trick of mixing clay and water to make soft gray walls.

We know a fair amount about Sarah as housekeeper because her husband was a paper saver. He kept old bills and shopping lists, stitching them together into handmade notebooks in which he copied out his sermons on the unused side of the paper. Because his sermons were saved, we have a record of the everyday details of his family's life together.

Other clergy soon learned to time their journeys cunningly so that nightfall brought them in the vicinity of Northampton. In those days there were few decent accommodations for travelers, yet ministers traveled widely in connection with their duties for clergy organizations which governed not only the religious affairs of a region but its political structure as well. Many men discovered that there was superior hospitality on King Street in Northampton.

Among Sarah's first callers in town were Madame John Stoddard and her daughters, who owned the first hoopskirts ever
seen in the region and had caused amazement when they had
first swished out in them. One reason Sarah was able to cope
smoothly with even such stylish guests was her extraordinary
good fortune as an employer. Early on, a colored servant named
Ruth came out from Boston to join the Edwards household.
She stayed contentedly for many years. The diaries and letters
of that era are full of complaints about how restless servants
became away from the excitement of cities. Other housekeepers on the frontier looked enviously at the durable Ruth.

The weather that fall provided a curious descant to their
honeymoon months. It swung to spooky extremes. In September there were unusually high winds. Then on October 29
an earthquake terrified New England with flashes of bluish
flames running along the ground. In spite of the weird weather,
work on the house continued. Edwards, recalling the elms of
New Haven, planted one on his own lawn, and it was to be
a town landmark for many years.

The most important moment in finishing the house was
raising the fireplace, the heart of the home and the literal
difference between life and death in the brutal Massachusetts
winter weather. The largest bedroom nestled against one warm
wall of the chimney core. In the attic, meat and grain were
dried in a warm room by the chimney. In the kitchen, apples,
onions, and pumpkins were hung to dry in the pungent warmth
of the hearth. It was a good symbol for a family to live around,
that single source of warmth and life, necessary to them all.

When one is falling in love, just to glimpse the other person
catches the breath, quickens the pulse. The touch of the precious person brings a rush of response from flesh and heart.
To have known such a period is to have lived in the mood of
an armistice day after a war—to be totally responsive, with
emotion close to the surface. But after marriage comes familiarity. In the case of the Edwardses, familiarity bred respect.
The real test of the feeling of one person for another is in the

daily encounters, when one must pay bills, carry out the trash, sniffle through a head cold. This period of homely testings disclosed to the couple that they were permanently committed to one another. So they turned now to translating their love into work, into a way of life.

One of the first facts Sarah had to become accustomed to was her husband's habit of waking at a horrendously early hour. Most people rose early because their routine was timed by the clockwork of animals. The cow had to be milked. Chickens went to roost. Dew took a certain length of time to evaporate before hay could be cut. But Edwards had so much to do that he sprang out of bed before most other people did. He had noted in his journal in January, 1728, "I think Christ has recommended rising early in the morning by his rising from the grave very early."

So everyone in the house was routed out, even in the dark winter dawns, for prayers by candlelight. With the servants joining in, they all heard a chapter from the Bible and asked God's blessing on the day ahead. Edwards continually watched for ways to squeeze the most out of every minute, as he put it: "Resolved never to lose one moment of time, but to improve it in the most profitable way I can." He fretted over time spent on journeys and soon was to work out an amusing way to grab even those hours on horseback.

As earnest about getting exercise as he was about everything else, he made a point of working for half an hour every day. In summer he would mend fences, inspect the sheep, putter in the garden. In winter he chopped wood. In that period all men took pride in their ability to handle an ax. Some were so skilled that they could smooth a wood surface until it looked planed, and even the cerebral Edwards enjoyed a good sweaty session of chopping wood.

However, Sarah had most of the responsibility for the property. She saw that the garden was planted, that the hired man had his instructions for each day. They used to tell in Northampton how once Edwards asked, "Isn't it about time the hay

was cut?" To which Sarah mildly replied, "It's been in the barn
for two weeks."

Very soon she became accustomed to his undependability
about appearing at meals. On January 22, 1734, he wrote: "I
judge that it is best when I am in a good frame for study . . .
that ordinarily I will not be interrupted by going to dinner, but
will forego my dinner, rather than be broke off." When he *did*
come to the table he was likely to vanish from the group
mentally, for even so small a matter as the choice between
beets or turnips from the ample table would propel him into
a chain of reasoning about freedom of the will. Some evenings
he would skip the meal the family had and eat bread and milk
instead, because he felt he needed the extra discipline.

She learned that he was unpredictable in his moods, swiftly
switching from intense creativity to paralyzed slumps. As he
confided to his journal: "I have had very affecting views of my
own sinfulness and vileness; very frequently to such a degree
as to hold me in a kind of loud weeping . . . so that I have
often been forced to shut myself up."

The town saw Edwards' composed dignity. Only his wife and
closest friends knew what storms slammed about inside the
controlled exterior of him.

What was driving him? He had to prepare a weekly Thursday evening lecture on the Bible, and two long Sunday sermons.
These products were models of reason and rhetorical power,
but they were more. Though the people in Northampton did
not realize it, they were witnessing a great mind pushing out
the frontiers of thought almost as drastically as other men in
that day were pushing back the forests.

The family's friend, Samuel Hopkins, has left a close account
of how the partnership of Jonathan and Sarah functioned:

> It was a happy circumstance that he could trust every-
> thing . . . to the care of Mrs. Edwards with entire safety
> and with undoubting confidence. She was a most judicious
> and faithful mistress of a family, habitually industrious, a

sound economist, managing her household affairs with diligence and discretion.

While she uniformly paid a becoming deference to her husband and treated him with entire respect, she spared no pains in conforming to his inclination and rendering everything in the family agreeable and pleasant; accounting it her greatest glory and there wherein she could best serve God and her generation, to be the means in this way of promoting his usefulness and happiness.

A genius is seldom an easy husband. When the great man is one who never looks at another woman, he is in some ways more taxing than a roving titan would be. A Tolstoy broke his wife's heart, but at least she was spared the full force of his stormy temperament. Other women also listened to his outpourings of elation or gloom, and deflected the lightning of his passions. But all of Edwards' heights and depths were brought to his wife. The object of such concentrated attention probably reached peaks of illumination few women do, but she must also have been singularly drained.

Though this relationship required more than does an attachment to a tamer man, Sarah had unusual compensations. Her husband treated her as a fully mature being—as a person whose conversation entertained him, whose spirit nourished his own religious life, whose presence gave him repose. For the first years of this highly charged marriage, Sarah bloomed.

About four o'clock on fair afternoons, Edwards would emerge from his study and suggest that Sarah join him for a horseback ride. Women then had a riding habit designed with a skirt elongated on the left side to hang over the stirrup as they rode demurely sidesaddle. Over the dress went a long coat, and in soggy weather flat clogs were added as overshoes. After Sarah had put on all this gear the couple would ride together in the hills above the river. Edwards would test the day's harvest of ideas against Sarah's practical intelligence, or he would talk over a parish problem with her. Perhaps they would simply jog along without speaking, but communicating.

She often visited him in his study, and at night they had prayers together after everyone else in the household had gone to bed. As their days began with thanks to God for the return of the miracle of morning, so they ended with the consecration of their sleeping selves to the Lord of both their lives.

On August 25, 1728, a Sunday, Sarah had a baby girl "between two and three in the afternoon," as Edwards wrote in the family Bible. He gladly made it his own task, one he took with high seriousness so that it was almost a sacramental gesture, to record the arrival of each child in that Bible. The first baby he chose to name Sarah. With the event of her birth began a procession of eleven children who gave Sarah Edwards her second great role.

# IV

## "Heaven Is a World of Love"

> The strength of the generations . . . depends on the
> process by which the youths of two sexes find their re-
> spective identities, fuse them in love or marriage, revitalize
> their respective traditions, and together create and "bring
> up" the next generation.
>
> —Erik H. Erikson

Quietly carrying the drudgery that freed her husband to
study, Sarah Edwards also managed to train a brood of children
whose social contribution is a phenomenon of American history.
In 1900, A. E. Winship tracked down fourteen hundred of their
descendants and published a study of the Edwards children in
contrast to the Jukes family, the notorious clan who cost New
York State a total of $1,250,000 in welfare and custodial charges.
Jukes wasn't actually the name of the other family. The word
means "to roost," and it was used about them because the
family were social floaters, with no home or nest. They all
originated with one immigrant who settled in upstate New
York in 1720 and produced a tribe of "idleness, ignorance, and
vulgarity."

Winship learned that a descendant of the Edwardses presided over the New York Prison Commission in 1874 when it
conducted an inquiry into the Jukes matter. Only 20 of the
1,200 Jukes had ever had gainful employment (the others were
either criminals or lived on state aid), whereas the Edwards

family had contributed astonishing riches to the American
scene. "Whatever the family has done it has done ably and
nobly," Winship contended. "And," he went on, "much of the
capacity and talent, intensity and character, of the more than
1,400 of the Edwards family is due to Mrs. Edwards."

By 1900 when Winship made his study, this single marriage
had produced

> 13 college presidents
> 65 professors
> 100 lawyers, and a dean of an outstanding law school
> 30 judges
> 66 physicians and a dean of a medical school
> 80 holders of public office:
> > three United States senators
> > mayors of three large cities
> > governors of three states
> > a Vice-President of the United States
> > a controller of the United States Treasury.

Almost all the men had college degrees and many completed
graduate work in a time when this was unusual. The women
were repeatedly described as "great readers" or "highly intelligent," although girls were not sent to college then. Members of
the family wrote 135 books, ranging from *Five Years in an
English University* to a tome on *Butterflies of North America*.
They edited eighteen journals and periodicals. They entered the
ministry in platoons and sent one hundred missionaries over-
seas, as well as stocking many mission boards with lay trustees.
One maverick married the daughter of a South Sea Island
chieftain but even that branch reverted to type, and its son
became a clergyman.

As Winship put it: "Many large banks, banking houses and
insurance companies have been directed by them. They have
been owners or superintendents of large coal mines . . . of
large iron plants and vast oil interests . . . and silver mines.
. . . There is scarcely any great American industry that has
not had one of this family among its chief promoters. . . . The

family has cost the country nothing in pauperism, in crime, in hospital or asylum service; on the contrary, it represents the highest usefulness."

The line still continues to be vigorous, intelligent, enlivening to society. Yet all this achievement came out of a family with no large inherited fortune. All the children's accomplishments were the result of their personal initiative.

This is not to blink at one naughty son and a grandson who was so sensationally shady that the Edwards traits seem to be printed on him in reverse, like the negative of a film. We will come presently to these stories. In each of these cases, however, the way the child turned out was the result of exterior circumstances, beyond the control of Sarah Edwards. Has any other mother contributed more vitality to the leadership of a nation?

How children turn out is always a reflection on their mother. In the Edwardses' case, where the mother had unusual responsibility for managing the household, the children are particularly revealing. Daughters catch their view of what it means to be a woman from their mother's view of her own femininity. The Edwards girls were exceptionally attractive to men, and fortunate in their choices of men to marry. (The talent for choosing the right mate is not one that distinguishes every famous family.) Winship states that "the family has never lost tone through marriage, for its members have chosen men and women of like character and capacity."

Every account of the Edwards house has the same ring. All visitors seem to have been impressed that eleven children managed to be lively and individual as personalities, yet could act courteously with one another and function as a coordinated unit. There may be a key to the many puzzlements of a parent today in a scrutiny of the way Sarah Edwards helped her children become strong characters. Her way was not at all permissive. The requirements were completely clear. But she at the same time allowed the children areas of flexibility that were unusual for that day, and she certainly managed to produce a line of remarkable people.

Sarah's first year with her first baby was not a promising start. On February 11, 1729, Solomon Stoddard died at the age of eighty-seven. He left £1,126, a library of 462 volumes, ten knives, nine forks, and a large hole in the town. A personality as decisive as Stoddard's changes a community by his departure from it. Edwards said of his grandfather that the leaders of Northampton "imitated his manners, which were dogmatic, and thought it an excellency to be like him." Straining to fill Stoddard's place, Edwards pushed so strenuously that he collapsed in May and had to go down to New Haven for a rest. The hardest force for a young minister to meet is torpor. Edwards wrote about this period: "Just after my grandfather's death it seemed a time of extraordinary dullness." It made Edwards feel that he had somehow failed. He brooded. He was hard to live with. In his effort to speak for God to the prickly people of Northampton, he had not yet learned to let God do a little of the work too.

The second Sarah was just beginning to lurch around on fat baby legs when another child was on the way. It caused jokes in town when this baby, too, arrived on a Sunday. Some ministers in those days refused to baptize children born on Sunday because it was believed that children arrived on the same day of the week that they had been conceived. The village wits enjoyed their speculations about their sedate minister when on April 26, 1730, "towards the conclusion of the afternoon exercise," the Edwardses acquired another daughter, Jerusha. Six Edwards children were to arrive conspicuously on a Sunday. There is still locked away in a collection of Edwards memorabilia at Princeton a christening blanket that once adorned Edwards himself and was used by all the children. It was the custom then to baptize children the Sabbath after birth. Legend has it that one of the Edwards children was baptized, red and squalling, when it was less than an hour old. It may have been Jerusha.

The birth of Jerusha was a landmark, because by now Dr. Samuel Mather was the town doctor. He had come to Northampton in 1728 to teach school, but after two years the town had persuaded him to be their doctor as well. How highly he was respected is indicated by the fact that he was appointed to the church's most august committees as well as to the school board. He was to be an important friend of the family.

Sarah sat up the day after the delivery to greet neighbors who stopped in for a bite of "groaning cake"—a pastry so named because it was served after labor. Every Sunday afterward she bundled her babies off to church. From their earliest days, Puritan babies had to accept those tedious hours in the meeting-house. Wearing linen dresses that Sarah had made and the heavy caps that were inflicted on small children winter and summer, the minister's children learned to be on view.

By the time Jerusha was big enough to play with her older sister, Sarah was pregnant again. It was a disappointment that she was not able to go along with her husband to Boston for his first triumph on July 8, 1731. He had been invited to give the Public Lecture, a special honor. As Perry Miller has described it:

> We may indeed be certain that all ministers not bed-ridden or in their dotage, together with the President, professors and tutors of Harvard College, as well as many substantial citizens were at hand. This was no routine performance. . . . [It was] the first time so large a collection of Harvard men . . . had an opportunity to take the measure of a Yale education.

The town of Northampton recognized the luster of the invitation that had come to their young parson, and had supplied him with £3 for his expenses for the trip to Boston. The Public Lecture was a day of utmost excitement in that city of thirteen thousand people. Crowds thronged on the Boston Common to have a glimpse of the young grandson of the mighty Stoddard, the man who had once dared to contradict Cotton Mather. Edwards had given lapidary attention to his manuscript, rehearsing it with Sarah, and he did well. The Boston ministers "congratulated the happy church at Northampton on whom Providence had bestowed so rich a gift."

Best of all, the sermon was printed. This chance to go into

print for the first time started Jonathan Edwards on his way to international renown.

In the aftermath of that triumph, the family had a happy year, and the baby who joined them on February 13 (just before church services) was a reflection of the vibrancy of that year. Hopkins has described this daughter:

> She exceeded most of her sex in the beauty of her person, as well as in her behavior. She had a lively, sprightly imagination . . . an uncommon degree of wit and vivacity . . . and she knew how to be facetious and sportive without trespassing on the bounds of decorum. . . . In short she seemed formed to please. . . . She was in every respect an ornament to her sex.

The child was named Esther after two other remarkable ladies. One was Edwards' vigorous mother. A second Esther was his grandmother, Stoddard's widow, who lived on actively, though she was lame, until she was ninety-two. She had fifteen children, twelve by Stoddard and three by her first husband, who had been Stoddard's predecessor in the Northampton church. When she had been first widowed, three church members went to Boston to look over the crop of Harvard graduates, hoping to persuade one to come to the Northampton church. Stoddard, son of a rich merchant, was about to sail to England, but the committee persuaded him to change his plans. They also allowed Esther to go on living in the parsonage with her children, so the church soon had not only a preacher but one with a wife. The child who received the name of these two ladies was to prove a memorable person in her own right.

With the advent of the third Esther there emerged a distinctive pattern of family life in the house on King Street. Edwards believed that "heaven is a world of love," and he found confirmation of this in his own house. Samuel Hopkins, who spent many months in the family, recalled of Sarah as a mother:

> She had an excellent way of governing her children; she knew how to make them regard and obey her cheerfully,

without loud angry words, much less heavy blows. She seldom punished them; and in speaking to them, used gentle and pleasant words. If any correction was necessary, she did not administer it in a passion; and when she had occasion to reprove and rebuke she would do it in few words, without warmth and noise. . . . In her directions in matters of importance, she would address herself to the reason of her children, that they might not only know her . . . will, but at the same time be convinced of the reasonableness of it. She had need to speak but once; she was cheerfully obeyed; murmuring and answering again were not known among them.

In their manners they were uncommonly respectful to their parents. When their parents came into the room they all rose instinctively from their seats and never resumed them until their parents were seated; and when either parent was speaking . . . they were all immediately silent and attentive. The kind and gentle treatment they received from their mother, while she strictly and punctiliously maintained her parental authority, seemed naturally to . . . promote a filial respect and affection, and to lead them to a mild tender treatment of each other. Quarrelling and contention, which too frequently take place among children, were in her family unknown.

Hopkins, the impressed house guest, goes on:

She carefully observed the first appearance of resentment and ill will in her young children, towards any person whatever, and did not connive at it . . . but was careful to show her displeasure and suppress it to the utmost; yet not by angry, wrathful words, which often provoke children to wrath. . . . Her system of discipline was begun at a very early age and it was her rule to resist the first, as well as every subsequent exhibition of temper or disobedience in the child . . . wisely reflecting that until a child will obey his parents he can never be brought to obey God.

A mother's disciplinary role was uncomplicated by the Freudian insight then. Moreover, the entire social structure supported parental authority. A child who felt free to be insolent toward parents was as unthinkable in that society as was the internal combustion engine. In such a context, it was not outlandish of Edwards to have written, as a Yale undergraduate: "Resolved never to allow the least measure of fretting or uneasiness at my father and mother . . . so much as in the least alternation of speech or motion of my eye." He carried over into his own role as father this calm assumption that a parent knows best. Sarah's transactions with her children were reinforced because her husband treated her with total courtesy and serenely expected that each child would follow his example. A curious feature about the Edwards children is that this firmness did not squash individuality. One explanation for this may be found in Hopkins' comment: "For [her children] she constantly and earnestly prayed and bore them on her heart before God . . . and that even before they were born."

In the eighteenth century babies were put into "puddings," a soft bolster tied around the middle like a life jacket. In it a toddler could putter safely, unlikely to be hurt by a fall. Esther was still lurching about "in pudding" on April 7, 1734, when Mary arrived. It was "Sunday, the sun being about an hour and a half high in the morning." Mary, a tiny girl of immense energy, eventually became the mother of another formidably talented line of children. The Sunday cycle was interrupted on a Tuesday, August 31, 1736, "between two and three o'clock A.M." when candles were lighted in the house and Lucy arrived. Then on July 25, 1738, when the household was already enlarged by a student living with them, a boy at last was born.

That all eleven Edwards babies lived is in itself remarkable. In that period, in some sections of London, infant mortality touched 100 percent. Thomas Clap wrote of his young wife:

> She would sometimes say to me that bearing, tending and burying children was hard work and that she had done a great deal of it. (She had six children whereof she buried four and died in the twenty-fourth year of her age) yet would say it was the work she was made for.

Ezra Stiles had ten children and only four lived. (He himself never forgot his shock when he was six years old and watched his baby brother expire just as his mother was dressing him to go to church.) Cotton Mather had fifteen children, and only two lived. Judge Sewall had fourteen, and only three survived. That all the Edwards babies thrived in such precarious times is a comment on Sarah's instinctive sense of nutrition, her clean house, and her good health during pregnancy. This may have caused jealous twinges among other mothers in the town who were not so blessed.

The management of a large, busy household took leadership and efficiency. Mothers then had to be administrators, because the food and clothing depended on the mother's ability to produce it. Sarah had to learn to assign chores so that one child would take a turn breaking ice in the lean-to next to the kitchen, to get water for the breakfast tea, while another child brought in wood. Meanwhile, if a guest was leaving after breakfast, someone else would be packing a lunch for his saddlebag. (A staple for such lunches was "journeycake"—a cornmeal concoction.) Another girl would be setting the table. Many households of that time were content to call a shot of hot buttered rum "breakfast," but the Edwardses sat down to large meals: bean porridge with ham bone, or cold corned beef and hot potatoes, or salt fish in cream. Cooking eggs was complicated because few houses had clocks. Eggs were sometimes timed by singing psalms. (An eight-line verse was usually right for boiling an egg.) The first cure for scurvy wasn't discovered until 1747, and this diet deficiency disease weakened many people, but there was none of it in Sarah's house. A prudent mother was also skeptical of drinking water. Many mothers found it safer to give babies beer, though one eighteenth-century almanac advised that it was "best to have their beer a little heated."

Children then had the advantage of knowing that their chores were indispensable. The smallest boy could help by watching a roast so that it browned evenly over the fire. Chickens and geese had to be fed. Fires had to be kept going twenty-four hours a day, for there were no matches. If a fire was allowed to go out, it was necessary to borrow from a neighbor to avoid having to start it again by tediously scraping flint against wood.

The Edwardses saw that the children learned to be orderly about money. The family Bible contains a record of the savings of each child, with receipts, expenditures, and borrowings neatly recorded. Sarah, according to Hopkins,

> was conscientiously careful, that nothing should be wasted and lost; and often, when she herself took care to save any-thing of trifling value, or directed her children or others to do so, or when she saw them waste any thing, she would repeat the words of our Savior—"THAT NOTH-ING BE LOST."

Sarah taught the girls to knit, embroider, and quilt. (Lucy once commented that making a quilt would be "very dull happiness to undertake alone.") They all took turns at the loom, and each girl seems to have developed her specialty in the housework. Esther gardened. Mary claimed that she was the champion maker of chocolate. The family consumed this treat in such quantities that most of Edwards' shopping lists con-tained a reminder to buy chocolate. The house functioned efficiently because all of these highly individual children were taught to work together.

This is not to say that the household was idyllic. There were the normal clashes and jostlings of ego that might be found in any large family. Sarah, the oldest girl, was peppery. Mary, a black-eyed bundle of vivacity, had a short-fused temper and a piercing voice that could grate on the nerves. She had another weakness. She was terrified of thunderstorms, and would dive into a featherbed for the duration of the storm. She took after her father, who reported, "Before, I used to be uncommonly terrified with thunder, and to be struck with terror when I saw a thunderstorm rising; but now, on the contrary, it rejoices me." Even when Mary was grown, and herself the mother of a large brood, she would gather them all with her, and quake in a featherbed when thunder rumbled. Esther was sometimes tactless, Jerusha nosy. A letter written to Susanna from Sarah in 1760 told a confidence and ended, "If you let any creature see this letter I shall never forgive you, burn it as soon as you've read it." That the letter wasn't burned says that "Sukey," too, had her streak of orneriness.

Esther, though charming, could be touchy. Mary once warned Lucy about her: "You know she never could bear pestering very well . . . so mind what you say." There were probably spats over whose turn it was to weed the carrots, or who used all the hot water washing her hair. Edwards spoke from experience when he wrote: "As innocent as children seem to be to us, yet . . . they are naturally very senseless and stupid, being born as the wild ass's colt, and need much to awaken them."

Family quarrels have a peculiar intensity because they bring back accumulated memories and grudges. Sharp exchanges with the members of one's own family hurt more than other controversies, for these are people most deeply involved with us. Yet out of the collection of thirteen explosive talents, ambitions, and energies, Sarah Edwards managed to mold that delicate structure, a family spirit. The word "ecology" comes from the Greek word for "house." Now it is used to describe "the manifold reciprocal relations of the organism to its natural surroundings." The Edwards household makes clear the connection between the root of the word and its contemporary usage. The members of her family functioned as an interdependent, balanced, flexible living organism.

The ways the children learned to cooperate with one another were not always jolly. There were many tedious household chores to do in those days. In the spring, four-poster beds had to be taken apart, the ropes reassembled, the canvas bottoms washed, the brown-linen sacking filled with clean straw. The children's clothes were made from homegrown wool, which had to be tediously combed, washed, and dyed. Sarah, like all frugal housekeepers, saved the purple wrapping paper whenever they had the rare and costly white sugar, and used it for a dye.

She made yellow by boiling certain barks. Soapmaking was a notably disagreeable task. The grease and lye, cooked together outdoors in a big iron pot, had a memorable smell, and the whole mess had to be stirred as it boiled. Another busy time for all hands in the house came in September when everyone pitched in to pick plums, quinces, and pears to make jam. Because the Edwardses used many candles, there was always the job of dipping candles, frugally scraping drips off the board to use again.

One source of the family stability was the steady dependable routine of prayers which they had together, before breakfast and again after supper. Edwards' choice of Scripture to read at these times is revealing: he was partial to the poetic books of the Bible—the psalms, Paul's passage on charity, the homely advice of Ecclesiastes. The surge and thunder of the King James Bible, heard twice a day aloud in their father's voice, became part of the children's earliest memories.

Edwards, though an absentminded father, gave his children another important thing: complete confidence that their parents loved each other. Sarah sat next to her husband at the table, and he treated her with great courtesy. She, in turn, leaned on him. Hopkins wrote:

> When she foresaw, or met with any special difficulty
> . . . she was wont to apply to her husband for advice and
> assistance and on such occasions they would both attend
> to it, as a matter of the utmost importance.

The parents approached the discipline of their children as a united pair, and this may be one reason why the children, in turn, married happily.

Sarah could also count on one hour a day when Edwards gave the family complete attention. He made sure to save an hour at the close of each day to spend with the children. Hopkins describes his

> entering freely into the feelings and concerns of his chil-
> dren and relaxing into cheerful and animate conversation

accompanied frequently with sprightly remarks and sallies
of wit and humor . . . then he went back to his study
for more work before dinner.

This was his hour to unbend completely. He enjoyed a
long pipe, and twice within one three months' period, ordered a
dozen of them. (This is a lapse in the usual Edwards rectitude,
for the General Court had ordered that no one should smoke
tobacco even in his own house "with a relative or friend.") The
children knew they could save their questions and have their
father's full attention at that precious hour when, without his
wig and smoking his pipe, he was a different man from the one
the parish usually saw.

Every Puritan house had one chair with a high back, which
was unmistakably the father's. No one else presumed to sit in
it—a fact that indicates a good deal about the clear outlines of
family order in those days. Father's place was unquestioned.

While Edwards would be sitting at his ease, Sarah might be
finishing a dress for one of the girls, Mary perhaps passing some
of her hot chocolate, and the smaller children sitting by the
fire making birch brooms of a design the settlers had picked up
from the Indians. (A large, active house with many fireplaces
needed constant sweeping.) The scene was similar to one described by Harriet Beecher Stowe, writing in 1859: "Perhaps
you remember your grandmother's floor of snowy boards sanded
with whitest sand. You remember the ancient fireplace stretching quite across one end—a vast cavern in each corner of which
a cosy seat might be found distant enough to enjoy the crackle
of the great jolly wood-fire . . . o that kitchen of the olden
times, the old, clean, roomy New England kitchen! Who that
has breakfasted, dined and supped in one has not cheery visions."
(The Minister's Wooing [Houghton Mifflin Company], p. 13.)

Edwards would use this relaxed hour to hear one child's
lessons. He had the idea, unusual in those times, that girls as
well as boys should be educated. In 1647 a Massachusetts law
insisted that each settlement of over fifty householders had to
provide a school for boys. So Northampton had a school, pre-

sided over by Samuel Allis, where the Edwards boys studied. The girls, tutored by their father at home, learned Latin, Greek, rhetoric, and penmanship. (They appear to have inherited their mother's frailty as a speller, however.)

Edwards also expected all the children to know Jewish and church history, the chronology of Biblical events, and how to correlate passages in the Old and New Testaments. A child never knew when, at the dinner table, he would be called upon to give a crisp answer to some such question as "How long was it after the destruction of Jerusalem by Nebuchadnezzar until Babylon was destroyed by Cyrus?"

The ubiquitous "Now I Lay Me Down to Sleep" first appeared in the New England primer in 1737. But Edwards did not encourage his children to lean on this doggerel, for he expected them to compose their own prayers. These children were exposed to the dark view of the riskiness of life, as this prayer expressed it, but the mood of the family seems to have been open, gay, humorous. The children were taught to fear God, but not to quake before him.

Though their behavior was bounded by strict rules, the girls had unusual freedom. The Northampton ladies marveled at how much each girl was allowed to travel. Edwards tried to take a daughter with him on each trip, letting the child ride on the pillion—the cushion behind the saddle. (He probably owned a Narraganset pacer, a breed of horse that had an unusually broad back, suitable for pillions.) Little Sarah went to the Massachusetts clergy meeting in 1743 when her mother was unable to go. She was allowed to visit her aunt when she was thirteen, and her father sent her a fond letter saying that her mother would let her have thread and bobbins if she wished to make lace during her free minutes on the trip.

Thanks to the fact that Mary, aged fifteen, went to Portsmouth, New Hampshire, ahead of her father to meet him when he came up for an engagement there, we have an amusing anecdote.

She told how Edwards was late in arriving, and thereby sent into a swivet Samuel Moody of York, Maine, a "gentle man of unquestioned talents and piety but perfectly unique in his manner." Mr. Moody had agreed to substitute for Edwards, should he be delayed. When Edwards did not arrive in time for the service, they delayed the Council. Poor Mr. Moody, trying to stall, offered an interminable prayer, covering every possible aspect of the absent speaker, and making supplications for his safety.

During the prayer, Edwards slipped in "so silently Mr. Moody did not hear him; and of course was necessitated, before a very numerous audience to listen to the very high character reference given to him" by the desperate Mr. Moody. When Moody at last turned around, he saw Edwards, and said:

> "Brother Edwards we are all of us much rejoiced to see you here today and nobody, probably, so much so as my-self. . . . I didn't intend to flatter you to your face, but there's one thing I'll tell you; they say your wife is going to heaven by a shorter road than yourself."

Edwards, typically, did not know how to make a light reply to this, so he just bowed.

Mary again went visiting in Boston, and Edwards wrote her an affectionate letter, full of advice about her soul, but also admonishing her to be sure to take advantage of any invitations she might receive.

The fact of living in so lovely a valley also affected the tone of the family. Mary's son was to love the Connecticut River so much that he remarked: "People who live on a pleasant surface and on a soil fertile and easy of cultivation usually possess softer dispositions and manners." The river curved in great oxbows, down a series of twenty-two terraces formed by ancient geological action, and it opened wide views of hill and meadow. It also provided excitement. The day the first shad appeared was always a celebration, for it meant a delectable change of menu after the dreary winter diet. There was another great day in spring, when flights of passenger pigeons winged up the river, fat from stuffing on southern grain. They would pass in such immense numbers that the day would be clouded, and the whole town would turn out in a carnival mood, and in expectation of pigeon pie. To help pay for covered bridges, lotteries were held, with the local minister expected to sanctify the drawing by a prayer.

Sheepshearings were other lively social occasions. All the sheep in the region were washed in a common pond, and shearers and drivers would turn up from out of town, full of news and jokes from outside. The Edwardses kept sheep, as all their neighbors did, so they shared in this excitement.

The boys played with tops and horseshoes, the girls joined in tag, and everyone enjoyed winter sports, coasting and skating. In the summer, carrying light baskets which the Indians had shown the settlers how to make, the children organized berry-picking parties in the folds of the little mountain near the town. They had good times, but no Edwards child was allowed out after nine o'clock. Other children in the village were, but Edwards, according to Hopkins, "thought the excuse offered by many parents, for tolerating this practice in their children . . . was insufficient and frivolous."

The clear restrictions the family imposed did not discourage swarms of beaux from the Edwards girls.

> If any gentleman desired to address . . . his daughters . . . he was allowed all proper opportunities of becoming thoroughly acquainted with the manners and disposition of the young lady but must not intrude on the customary rest and sleep nor on the religion and order of the family. (Hopkins.)

Edwards managed to pull it off because he combined consistency with his firmness. He admonished parents: "Take heed that it may not be with any of you as it was with Eli of old who *reproved* his children, but *restrained* them not." (Italics added.)

Edwards followed another sound psychological principle, saying:

> There is such a thing as anger that is consistent with good will. A father may be angry with his child . . . yet

at the same time he will not have any proper ill-will to the child.

The Edwardses made it a point to single out individual children from the humming family hive, to get to know each one in turn by himself. ("He took opportunities to converse with them singly and closely.") They also did much letter-writing between members of the family. Now, though families may be widely scattered, few make the effort to capture their life, routine, and thoughts for their relatives at a distance. Edwards believed in letter-writing not only because it knitted a family together, but because he saw it as a device for teaching children to write easily.

Perhaps the most formative feature in the development of these children was the sense of privilege they felt, as a minister's family, on the great occasion of Sunday. Puritans toiled hard all week, so they took seriously the admonition to rest on the Sabbath. After sundown on Saturday no one could work at all, except to brush sparks from the hearth. They couldn't even make beds. So a Puritan housewife shined up her house on Saturday, and did a colossal baking. Then after three o'clock on Saturday afternoon, the mood of expectancy began to build up to the pivotal day. These people really believed that Sunday would bring encounter with a living and dependable God who had brought them to this new land and watched over their effort to build his holy commonwealth.

While a large roast cooked all day, to ensure cold meat for Sunday, a great copper tub before the fire held water which was being warmed for baths. Shoes were shined, clothes laid out for the next day, and "modesty pieces" ironed. (These were inserts of lace or velvet that were tucked into the neckline of a Sunday dress. Drafts as much as discretion made them a sensible fashion accessory.) Father, abstracted, would be finishing his two sermons for the next day. Then on Saturday night the family sang a psalm together, had prayers, and went upstairs to bed with a sense of anticipating drama, as children now do only on Christmas Eve. Edwards tells us: "One Saturday night in

particular I had such a discovery of the excellence of the gospel
. . . that I could not but say to myself: 'This is my chosen
Prophet.' It appeared sweet, beyond all expectation."

Sarah's way with their children did more for Edwards than
shield him from hullabaloo while he studied. The family gave
him incarnate foundation for his ethic. As George Gordon has
put it, Edwards' life at home opened up "the world in which
love lifts the whole animal endowment to an ethical level." In
1738, Edwards poured out his feelings about this in sermons
which eventually appeared as a book, *Christian Love as Mani-
fested in the Heart and Life*. There he summarized the conviction his family had planted in him that "the whole world of
mankind are chiefly kept in action from day to day . . . by
love." The last Sunday he stood in the Northampton pulpit as
pastor of the church, he put in this word for his people: "Every
family ought to be . . . a little church, consecrated to Christ
and wholly influenced and governed by His rules. And family
education and order are some of the chief means of grace. If
these fail, all other means are like to prove ineffectual."

Nothing nowadays is more ambiguous than the real motiva-
tion for altruism. All self-giving service is suspect, and that of
mothers is the most murky of all. To compound the puzzle, the
fundamental force of love is also challenged, and when we think
we are being loving we are told that we may be manipulating.
So we do not know what to think of Sarah Edwards' career of
love and giving. Can we, who scarcely understand the sub-
terranean reasons for our own actions, possibly probe the motives
of a woman who lived two centuries ago in an entirely different
social setting? She probably contained a mix of warring impulses, as everyone does. She was the noble mother for fourteen
years and then even this clear spirit was briefly shattered. When
she had passed through her crisis, she was more than ever
gentle and generous. Across the years and through all the ambigu-
ities, she forces us to consider the possibility that there may be
an occasional person who gives out of a simple overflow of holy
joy.

# V

## The Active Latchstring

She knew the heart of a stranger.
—*Samuel Hopkins*

If her offspring formed a monument to Sarah Edwards, so did her friendships. The effect of her hospitality reverberated through the lives of a number of people. At the entrance to Forbes Library in Northampton today is a worn little stone sunken into the grass. This was the doorstep to the Edwards house. Across it tramped the feet of so many visitors that the mind boggles at the thought of what was involved in bedding and feeding them all.

Those were days of dubious taverns, so most travelers counted on stopping with the ministers in whatever town they struck by night. As Edwards' reputation mounted, and the charms of his daughters became widely known, the number of guests grew. Moreover, in those times there were no seminaries, so men who wished to become clergymen lived as apprentices in the houses of experienced ministers. There was almost always some downy cleric at the Edwards fireplace. It is significant that the young men who lived with them most intimately became their stoutest friends.

The expression "The latchstring is out" dates to this period in history when doors had no locks, just a latch. If visitors were welcome, the string was left dangling outside. When the family did not choose to be disturbed, it was easy to pull the

string in. Those who pulled the Edwards latchstring seem to
have found Sarah a gifted hostess. As Hopkins recalled: "She
was peculiarly kind to strangers. . . . By her sweet and winning
manners and ready conversation she soon became acquainted
with them . . . and led him immediately to feel as if he were
at home." We get an idea of the constant dropping-in that went
on at the house on King Street from such reports as this one
from Sarah herself: "I heard him once speak on these things
very freely and fully . . . when Mr. Buel* and Mr. Osborn of
Long Island and Lt. Phelps and Mr. Noah Parsons of this town
were present and while he was discoursing on it, Noah Lyman
came in."

When the girls' beaux joined the traffic, there were times
when the walls bulged. Yet, according to Hopkins, Sarah
"[spared] no pains to make [guests] welcome and to provide for
their convenience and comfort." Edwards was less than helpful as a host, for he was still a light eater and would often finish
his meal before the others did. He would then slip out to his
study, returning to the table only when he was alerted that the
others had finished and he was needed to preside over the grace
which was always said at the end of meals as well as at the
beginning. Meanwhile, Sarah had to keep an eye on the children's table manners and on the supply of hot gravy, remember
the heating of water to wash dishes, and at the same time keep
conversation going with the guests. At the end of the meal a
basket was passed around the table and everything that had
been used, including napkins, was piled into it to be washed.
Sarah's work was not over when a big meal was consumed.

She cooked for large, fluctuating numbers of guests without
the help of light modern utensils. A family then might use iron
pots weighing forty pounds, and meals had many more courses
than we expect now. Without refrigeration, she had to learn
ways to save food, often by means of stews that could be brought

---

* Sarah was, as we have said, a shaky speller. The man's name was
really "Buell."

to a presumably sterilizing boil a second day. One aspect of cooking then was a joy. Several times a week a roaring fire would be encouraged at bedtime and a batch of dough then put into a sealed oven. In the morning, bread would be waiting, fragrant and crusty.

The Edwards house, like all houses of the period, had no closets, only pegs and chests. When guests clumped in and strewed around the contents of saddlebags, or perhaps had to dry out riding clothes after a sudden shower, the rooms seemed awash with belongings. Fortunately, even the most elegant people then did not consider privacy to be essential. When Sarah stretched her house to take in extra guests, she managed to give them a feeling that they had had an unusual experience. In her approach to housekeeping, efficiency was tempered by composure. She knew how to keep a house clean at its vitals, without stuffy cupboards left unaired or parlors sealed off. The house was open, used, full of clues that the family living in it had vivid interests. Books were left on tables, actually being read, not used as parlor props. There would be needlepoint on a rack by a sunny window and a lute in a corner. Esther, singing, might be putting up a hem for Sukey while a boy did his Latin lesson. It was the opposite of the kind of house where things were preserved in mothballs in locked boxes. Its ambience was of windows flung open, of easy welcome.

Because Sarah spent no time on gossip, she had the extra time that other women let leak away—a minute to place a pewter candlestick where it would be reflected in a mirror, time to make rose petals into a potpourri that would scatter fragrance through a sheet chest. She communicated this art of keeping house to her daughters, so that they, too, left visitors with an impression of a house with distinctive character.

In a large family, outside the general social life of the town, isolated by their intelligence and their singular position in the community, there was a quality similar to the atmosphere of isolated manor houses, a certain psychological closeness and intensity. When Jerusha would arrive home from a visit in

New Haven with her uncle James Pierrepont, the whole family
would sit down to hear her report. When Mary's beau stayed
for dinner or Esther came home from the pond with the news
that Timothy had managed to stand up on ice skates, the whole
family was involved. They needed one another and knew it.
Most essential of all was Sarah. Once when she was away,
Esther wrote a friend: "You can't conceive how everything
alters upon my mother going away. All is dark as Egypt."

The Edwardses enjoyed not only visiting with friends but
writing to them. Because Edwards needed to hone his ideas
against other competent intellects, and Northampton did not
offer many men of challenging mentality, he corresponded
widely. In those days it was an act of faith to mail a letter. The
government did not start systematic mail delivery until 1754.
In 1639 the state of Massachusetts had decided to stop "mis-
carriage of letters," so they arranged that all mail was to go to
the house of Richard Fairbanks, who thus informally became
postmaster. Boston was the only city with a system as methodical as that. Outside Boston, letters were usually just handed
casually to any traveler who happened to be headed in the ap-
proximate direction of the addressee. Often these couriers were
butchers who had to make trips to buy meat. Whenever Edwards
heard that a traveler had arrived in town from Philadelphia or
Boston, he would stroll down to the tavern by the river and
inquire if by any chance a letter had come for him.

Writing paper was scarce and costly. William Rittenhouse had
started the first paper mill in 1690 in Germantown, Pennsylvania, charging twenty shillings a ream for his products because
they were hard to make. Until envelopes came into use about
1839, letters were just folded and sealed with wax. The
Edwardses cherished correspondence so much that they were
formidable letter writers in spite of the cost, inconvenience,
and uncertainty.

In 1741 the wrought-iron knocker on the house in King
Street thudded at the touch of a diffident visitor who was to
leave an indispensable memoir of the Edwardses. He was

Samuel Hopkins, from Waterbury, Connecticut, where his mother was a member of the distinguished Judd family and his father was many times a delegate to the state's General Court. Hopkins had graduated from Yale and after he heard Edwards preach, he decided that he wished to study with him. So he rode up to Northampton and this is his report:

> When I arrived there, Mr. Edwards was not at home, but I was received with great kindness by Mrs. Edwards and the family and had encouragement that I might live there during the winter. Mr. Edwards was absent on a preaching tour. . . . I was very gloomy and was most of the time retired in my chamber. After some days, Mrs. Edwards came [in] . . . and said As I was now become a member of the family for a season, she felt herself interested in my welfare and as she observed that I appeared gloomy and dejected, she hoped I would not think she intruded her desiring to know and asking me what was the occasion of it. . . . I told her . . . I was in a Christless, graceless state. . . . Upon which we entered into a free conversation and . . . she told me that she had [prayed] respecting me since I had been in the family; that she trusted I should receive light and comfort and doubted not that God intended yet to do great things by me.

Sarah then had seven small children clamoring for her attention and her husband was away, but she took time to note the need of a gloomy young stranger. He never forgot this.

Hopkins carried away with him from the Edwards house their brand of Calvinism as well as some of the personal courage he admired in his teacher. In 1769, Hopkins became minister in Newport, Rhode Island, in a town that was prospering on a slave economy. (The temperate bay around Newport was the only area in chilly New England where slaves were used as field hands. In most other places they were house servants.) Before that congregation, Hopkins stood up and in his voice "like a cracked bell" challenged the morality of slavery. He also proposed a plan to educate slaves, free them and send them back to

Africa to help their own people. Some of Hopkins' hearers
bridled at this suggestion, but one young man was impressed.

William Ellery Channing, two years out of Harvard, was
floundering for a purpose in his life. "Thin and pallid," he had
come back to his hometown in discouragement. He had long
talks with Hopkins, pulled himself together, went back to
Boston, became a minister who influenced Emerson and
Thoreau. Channing also had a large part in the abolitionist
movement. So Sarah Edwards had a correct intuition that the
Lord had some purpose ahead for Hopkins, the boy she had encouraged.

Another apprentice preacher who spent a long period studying with Edwards was Joseph Bellamy, later the minister in
Bethlehem, Connecticut. (That was a delectable town where
in October yellow leaves gloriously carpeted the lanes, but
Bellamy did not find a spirit in the town equal to its scenery.
He muttered that "any true godliness [there] was apparently
practiced in the closet, there being no sign of it anywhere
else.")

During his eighteen months in Northampton, Bellamy picked
up high standards for preaching. When he in turn had to
supervise an apprentice, Bellamy listened quizzically while the
boy tried to cover the entire salvation scheme in a single
sermon. Then Bellamy asked the young orator, "Do you ever
expect to preach again?" Bellamy's reading taste was also affected by Edwards, who "was all his days like the busy bee,
collecting from every opening flower and storing up a stock of
knowledge." Edwards' interest in the secular mind rubbed off
on Bellamy. He bought "so much work by heretics" that his
library was hard to sell at auction after his death.

As Hopkins put it: "Among such whose candor and friendship
[Edwards] had experienced, he threw off the reserve and was
most open and free: quite patient of contradiction." The many
evenings Bellamy spent beside the Edwards fireside, bouncing
ideas back at the older man, were education in a profound
sense. When Edwards died, his great work on original sin was
still at the printer's. Bellamy saw it published, then carried

on a vigorous pamphlet defense of it when its ideas were challenged by some readers. Then when Jonathan Edwards, Jr., graduated from Princeton in 1765, Bellamy took him in as *his* student.

Once at an unusually busy point in his life, Edwards took time to explain a thorny passage of Scripture that Bellamy had inquired about. This brief note, of July 18, 1749, conveys some of the ease Edwards felt with Bellamy, and some of the humor he shyly showed to his friends:

> The printer in Boston told me my Book on the Sacraments would be done in about three weeks; that is, now next week. But I understand their language and don't expect it until the beginning of September. I am Sir, Your brother and Entire Friend.

One of the sunniest friendships was that of the whole Edwards family with the family of Thomas Prince, cominister of Old South Church in Boston. Old South was an influential church, and Prince was a man who enjoyed power and the good things of life in the vibrant Boston world. The new building of Old South, built in 1727, marked a new epoch in church architecture. It was perhaps the first example of what is now designated as the "colonial" style.

Prince was a Harvard graduate who had traveled abroad after college, met an English girl there, and married her. (She became a particular friend of Sarah's.) Called to Old South in 1718, Prince stayed forty years there, living in a charming house that had been Governor Winthrop's. The Edwardses often visited in this house, which unhappily was destroyed and used for firewood by the British during the winter of 1775.

The most famous story about Thomas Prince concerns the time forty French warships sailed to attack New England in the fall of 1746, during King George's War. The day was calm and sunny when Prince chose to pray in church:

> Send Thy Tempest, Lord, upon the waters to the Eastward. Raise thy right hand. Scatter the ships of our tormentors and drive them hence.

The day darkened; a violent wind came up. In the tempest that followed, the fleet was scattered and crippled. D'Anville, the commander, died. Later it was discovered that he carried an order to "lay [Boston] in ashes." On November 27, 1746, Prince acknowledged this in a sermon on "Divine Providence in the destruction of the French fleet and army."

Prince had a scholarly passion for organizing the history of the first century of the colonies, and compiled a valuable chronology of it. When John Adams visited the balcony of the church in 1811 he found Prince's book collection so irresistible that the catalogue of Adams' own library confesses that "it seems probable that on one or more of his visits to this balcony Mr. Adams borrowed these volumes and failed to return them."

Prince owned the irreplaceable manuscript of Bradford's *History of Plimouth Plantation*. It was tossed about carelessly during the Revolution and just escaped being used to kindle a fire when the church was occupied by the Queen's Light Dragoons as a riding rink. By some miracle, the manuscript wandered to London to the bishop of London's palace, where it was safe.

It was Thomas Prince who first introduced Edwards to a publisher. Edwards' daughters were friends of Sally Prince, and they continued to write to her for many years. Sally Prince married a Boston merchant, Moses Gill, who built a splendid country place on three thousand acres of land that Prince had picked up between Boston and Northampton, possibly on a ride back from a visit in the Edwards home. The town he started is still named Princeton.

No one reacted blandly to Edwards. He gave people a disturbing hunch that they were in the presence of a strangely different person. Sarah had sensed this and found it frightening when he first courted her. Clergymen who had settled for the routine, the safely popular options, resented a man like Edwards. His concentration repelled them. His moral force was a threat. But Prince was a man of nimble mind and distinct ability. He rejoiced at finding a companion like Edwards, and the men met as equals.

It never occurred to Edwards that he might have been snobbish, though he impressed some people that way. Edwards could be open and encouraging to an unimportant young clergyman like Jonathan Judd, who came to the nearby church of Southampton. Edwards took the trouble to ride down to Westfield, to escort Judd to his new post, then he preached the installation sermon for him. Similarly, long after Edwards' death it was learned that he had once heard of a "poor obscure man he never saw" who was in unusual need. Edwards, "unasked, gave a considerable sum to a friend, to be delivered to the distressed person," requesting that no one be told the donor's name.

Perhaps the most fascinating friendship of the Edwardses was with a group of people they never met. Though ocean travel was unpredictable and mail chancy, they built a circle of friends in Scotland. It happened this way. When Prince managed to get Edwards' first book published, several copies reached Scotland. Some Scottish ministers wrote to congratulate Edwards, and he wrote back enthusiastically, first to a Mr. McCulloch, of Cambuslang, then to a whole group. One of these, Mr. John Erskine, a man of private wealth, had chosen to be a minister against the wishes of his aristocratic family. As a pastor in Edinburgh, Erskine had been told about Edwards by Mr. McLaurin, of Glasgow, and he sent Edwards a memoir which he had written about a friend. Edwards replied warmly, beginning a friendship that was to leave many evidences of Erskine's generosity in the house on King Street. A picture of John the Evangelist on the living room wall was a gift from Erskine; so was a magnificent silver tankard, and many books. After Edwards died, Erskine continued to correspond with his son, and then with his grandson. Twelve of these Scottish ministers worked out a plan to join Edwards in prayer on a certain day. It may well have been the first World Day of Prayer.

What was involved in keeping up a correspondence abroad is revealed in letters from Edwards to McCulloch. Edwards had to rely on Thomas Prince to be a go-between, sending along letters to ships in the Boston Harbor. Mr. Prince was apparently more obliging than he was reliable, for Edwards commented in 1748:

> I wrote an answer to your letter [dated March 12, 1746] and sent it to Mr. Prince of Boston . . . and am very sorry that you never received it.

Again:

> I desired Mr. Prince of Boston to send you one of my books . . . soon after it was published; who engaged to do it but long forgot it.

And once more:

> I thank you for your letter which . . . lay a long while at Mr. Prince's in Boston before I received it. . . . It seems he had forgotten that he had any such letter. . . . I should probably never have had it at last had not one of my daughters . . . made a visit at the house and made a more full inquiry.

Evidently, Edwards bit his tongue and reminded himself of the good table conversation, the gaiety and respite that the Prince hospitality offered to all the Edwardses, because the friendship survived these small annoyances.

That Edwards never met his contemporary, Benjamin Franklin, is interesting. Franklin was educated a Presbyterian, and he confides in his *Autobiography*: "I never was without some religious principles. I never doubted, for instance, the existence of the Deity," but in the main he was more interested in this world than in the next. Edwards in contrast believed that "God was the Essence of Being, Supreme, Powerful, Grand." Like Edwards, Franklin in his youth kept a journal of fine resolves, but his entries ran more to such plans as this for ordering the day: "Rise, wash & address 'Powerful Goodness' . . . evening question: What good have I done today?" Franklin was an artist of compromise, a supreme politician, Edwards an execrable one. The men were also dissimilar in their marriages. Franklin's was never based on love. He was away in Europe for years at a time without causing pain either to himself or to his matter-of-fact wife. He thrived on flirtations. Edwards stayed totally absorbed all his life by one passion for one woman.

One of Franklin's maxims went: "Great Estates may venture more, But little Boats should keep near Shore." By keeping near shore, in the safe, observable, manipulable dimension, Franklin contributed a great deal of good: a peace treaty; a postal service; a fire company; a wondrous stove. Edwards rashly ventured far and he seemed in his lifetime to have been a failure. The two men were the largest figures of their period in American history, but it may be just as well that they never met. They might have disliked each other.

Those who did like the Edwardses were more than friends. They were their fierce partisans. Yet a person like Sarah Edwards had a risk in the very magnetism that pulled people to her. So many felt warmed by being around her that to meet the needs of all who wanted her attention would have taken superhuman energy from her. She seemed to make people feel that what they needed most was to sit down for a cup of tea with her, and tell her about themselves. How can one budget kindnesses, ration out one's concern for others? Though she felt the tension of never being able to give all that people wanted to take from her, Sarah Edwards continued to pour out all that she could. For many people a memory they carried with them always was of a time when they turned up the path to the Edwards door, and pulled the latchstring hanging there outside.

# VI

## What Was Driving Him?

> . . . Truly men hate the truth, they'd liefer
> Meet a tiger on the road.
> —From a poem by Robinson Jeffers, a
> descendant of Jonathan and Sarah Edwards

How can the occasional appearance of genius in the world be explained? Is it haphazard chance of some fortunate chemistry? or a plan of God—his way of nudging forward the history of mankind?

Edwards' mind strode far ahead of the thinking of his century as he worked out a complex theory of being that stressed "the congruity of God's action to man's situations." As a thinker, Edwards was one of the rare people who are able to hold ideas in suspension. He would retain a thought, turn it about, test it against another thought, tuning out the many distractions that scatter the attention of most people. Such a man reaches heights of exhilaration when he has a unifying insight, but he also probes depths most people prefer not to contemplate.

Sarah's way of handling such a husband was simply to let him be sure of her steady love, and then to free him to think. She meanwhile was the one who coped with the children's disagreements and thought of ways to use up yesterday's joint of lamb.

There are long shelves of commentary about the intellectual contribution of Edwards. It would be pretentious as well as redundant to try to deal with this subject here. But briefly, he was one of the first Americans to realize that the world was going through both a scientific and a psychological revolution. The upheaval in science came as a result of the work of Sir Isaac Newton. The new psychology had been voiced by John Locke. A 1690 edition of Locke appeared in the collection that Jeremiah Dummer had managed to acquire for Yale in 1713. Edwards came across it when he was a sophomore and "read it with more pleasure than the most greedy miser finds when gathering up handfuls of silver and gold from some newly-discovered treasure."

As late as 1746, Yale was still serenely teaching Aristotelian rhetoric, but Edwards had absorbed the new science. Alone in his study, he worked over the new ideas that beat against his brain. He asked: Why a world? He wrestled with the possibility that pesters modern, bomb-obsessed man, "God can shake all to pieces."

He studied nature because he was convinced that this world is God's world. He made a list he entitled "Things to be Observed." He made entries, complete with neat diagrams, on such questions as why bubbles break on the surface of water, why the heat of the sun is greater nearer the earth than at a distance from it, why waves move as they do and, Do atoms touch each other? He conjectured whether stars might be blazing suns attended by their own planets. In his interest in science, Edwards was not singular among the more learned clergy, however. Many of them were interested in science. Cotton Mather was a member of the Royal Society, and sent to them in 1714 specimens of fossil teeth and observations about moose. Paul Dudley, of Roxbury, Massachusetts, had written for the Royal Society an *Essay on the Natural History of Whales* and he also made a systematic study of earthquakes. But Edwards added a philosophic dimension to his observations on nature which made them unusual for that time.

When he was younger, Edwards had pondered how to make use of the time he had to spend on journeys. After the move to Northampton he worked out a plan for pinning a small piece of paper to a given spot on his coat, assigning the paper a number and charging his mind to associate a subject with that piece of paper. After a ride as long as the three-day return from Boston he would be bristling with papers. Back in his study, he would take off the papers methodically, and write down the train of thought each slip recalled to him.

As a social philosopher he tried to apply ethics to the actual situation of societies. He also pioneered in the theory of communication, anticipating to a remarkable degree the science of semantics. ("Resolved in narrations, never to speak anything but the pure and simple verity.") He toiled over his writing efforts until he met the requirement he had set for himself: "Extricate all questions from the least confusion by words or ambiguity of words so that the Ideas shall be left naked."

Edwards' fund of information had some curious gaps. Though Bach, Buxtehude, Vivaldi, Scarlatti, and other masters of baroque music had poured out their riches, there is no indication that Edwards was aware of their dimensions, or even that he appreciated the magnitude of Handel's *Messiah*, first heard in 1741. He seems to have been similarly spotty in his taste for the visual arts, though one might expect him to have commented upon Hogarth's *Rake's Progress* (1735). He was solidly grounded in history, but other men of his era were more aware of the significant political forces shaping up in the colonies, foreshadowing the mood of the Revolution.

All of his original intellectual contributions were mulched by reading. Back in Yale he began keeping a notebook reminding him of books he wanted to read, and he kept that up all his life. In many of the books in his collection are marginal notes scribbled beside certain passages, saying "out" or "written out," meaning that he had copied the passage. He followed the colorful careers of the Wesleys and made a point of acquiring the collection of hymns they had composed. It is not surprising that one of the few novels he bothered to read was Fielding's *Amelia*, which contains "the most exquisite figure of a woman that Fielding ever painted."

How did he acquire books in that day when books were not

common? He scrounged shamelessly. Once he persuaded the parish to give him a salary increase for books. He was a chronic borrower, and when books were the game, he forgot his shyness and went after the trophies he wanted. He enjoyed tracking down such rare items as the *Hier Osorius*, published in Cologne in 1584. It is now in Princeton Library, along with his Hebrew lexicon bound in otter skin. When he died, he left 336 volumes and 536 pamphlets, a considerable library for that era.

The Edwardses all enjoyed newspapers. The *Boston News-letter* had been started in 1704 by a postmaster who collected news by a stunningly simple device—he read the mail entrusted to him, then reinforced these stolen gleanings with items pried out of sea captains, sailors, and riders who came to town carrying the mail. In 1721, Benjamin Franklin's brother started the rival *New England Courant*. There was also a dullish, semiofficial *Boston Gazette*. In the margin of a copy of the *Gazette* for March 3, 1743, Edwards scribbled notes for a sermon outline.

Edwards methodically numbered all his writing. Each sheet was numbered in sequence, then entered under subject matter in a book he arranged alphabetically. Thus he could swiftly turn to a subject. For thirteen hours each day he would sit at his straight table, his sheaf of quills before him in a pewter cup. When daylight faded, he lighted a candle in a holder with curved iron branches and went on writing.

All the hours he spent in his study funneled into the solemn hours on Sunday when he stood before his people. Those who are acquainted only with Edwards' "spider" sermon ought to know that though he began with the reality of sin, he felt that the theme of redemption was central. Sunday after Sunday he pleaded with his people to accept the grace of God, which seemed to him to be so real.

It is instructive to notice what words a minister repeats oftenest. The noun that appeared most frequently in Edwards' work was "sweetness." To him, the gift of grace was sweet, and he longed to share it.

Though it wasn't done at the time, and Stoddard had publicly frowned on it, Edwards in the early years of his ministry preached from a manuscript. He wanted to be sure he said precisely what he meant to say, for he had no patience with slovenly ramblings. So he stitched together his pages of used shopping lists, making tiny books that he held in his left hand. (One, the size of a wallet, may be viewed at Princeton.) He used few gestures, and spoke in a low voice, with "great distinctness in pronunciation." Hopkins contends that

> the effect of it was to enable him to speak to the consciousness of every one who heard him so that each one was compelled to reflect . . . here is a man who is revealing to me the secrets of my own heart and life. . . . No man ever suspected him of writing a sermon for the display or reputation. . . . He aimed at nothing but the glory of God.

Edwards had some amusing quirks as a preacher. One sermon on "Jesus wept" he liked so much that he delivered it in six different towns and wrote in the margin "very good." He had trouble remembering the announcements he was supposed to make, so he wrote out reminders to himself in very large letters at the ends of sermons. (Some ministers even today are familiar with that problem.) He disappointed people because he seldom took note of local occasions. In our time he would not have taken pains to salute Mother's Day or Boy Scout Week, but he did weave current events into his sermons when the matter seemed sufficiently important to him. He mentioned the Proclamation of War with the Indians on September 19, 1745, and noted the arrival of the French fleet on October 16, 1746. When the courthouse burned, he remarked on that, and in August of 1749 he gave a special thanksgiving for rain, so essential for his farming congregation.

He disliked long prayers, observing that they tended "rather to damp than to promote true devotion." There probably were other clergy who bridled when he twitted "those modern fashionable discourses which are delivered under the name of sermons but really are mere harangues on such moral subjects as have been much better handled by Cicero, Seneca or the *Spectator*." What he wanted to express through preaching was what it may mean "to be full of Christ alone; to love him with a holy and true love; to trust in him; to live upon him." He saw humanity quarreling with one another, and resisting God, who longed to save them. But much of his eloquence went over the heads of the people in the Northampton pews. Thomas Hooker once had exploded:

> I have sometimes admired at this: why a company of Gentlemen, yeomen and poorewomen, that are scarcely able to know their ABC yet have a minister to speak Latine, Greek and Hebrew . . . when it is certain they know nothing at all. The reason is, because all this stings not. They may sit and sleep in their sins.

Edwards began to sting, and there began to be mutterings in the "Shabbaday House," the small building with fireplace and blankets, where people who lived at a distance could bring their box lunches and thaw out between the morning and afternoon services. Stretching after the long service, and warming their stiffened bottoms against the fire, the people remarked that the young minister might spend less time preparing sermons and make more calls around town, for Edwards did not do the affable, social calling that parishioners enjoyed. Dwight explains:

> He observed that some had a talent for entertaining. . . . [They had] a manner free, natural and familiar. . . . [But] he was not able to enter into a free conversation with every person . . . and in an easy manner. . . . He therefore found that his visits of this time must be . . . improfitable.

However, anyone with spiritual questions was free to visit *him* and Dwight assures us that when people visited Edwards in his study they were "treated with all desirable tenderness, kindness and familiarity." When Edwards did occasionally make a clumsy effort at the kind of jocular exchange that the people enjoyed, he was ludicrous. One of his grandsons liked to tell about the time Edwards went to his pasture for the cow when he was taking a breather for exercise at the end of a day of study. A small boy, seeing him coming, opened the gate, bowed, let him through. Edwards asked with dim kindliness, "Whose son are you?" "I am John Clark's boy, sir." When Edwards returned, the boy once more opened the gate. Edwards asked again, "Whose boy are you?" The reply was, "The same man's boy I was five minutes ago, sir."

Though Edwards did not make the trivial call just to be popular, he was right there with his people in time of genuine crisis. When the Lyman house burned and two children died, he gave the family full support, and even shaped his sermon for that week around the event. If a person's barn was struck by lightning, or a horse fell on a rider, or a neighbor was scalded during butchering, Edwards was a compassionate pastor. When the issues were large, the grief real, the choice critical, Edwards responded humanly to a human need. But most of the time, he studied.

Massively earnest and, it must be admitted, tactless, he plodded along, blasting at his congregation with passages like this:

> You who . . . sit here in these seats so easy and quiet and go away so careless—by and by you will shake and tremble and gnash your teeth and will be thoroughly convinced of the vast weight and importance of those things you now despise. You will not then need to hear sermons in order to make you sensible.

No one who feels comfortable with things as they are enjoys being told by one man of lonely insight that life could be more than they make of it. Preacher and people had begun to move along a collision course.

# VII

## The Awakening:
## A Dubious Blessing

Wild-fire has been mixed with it.
  —George Whitefield, to his Journal

A mighty wave of religious conviction had brought a new nation onto the North American continent, but now a century had passed and ennui had replaced holy fervor. People had gleefully begun to explore worldly diversions. Some were starting to question the stern grasp the church kept upon the social structure. Many were simply bored by religion. In that unpromising context, there began in 1734 in Northampton the first phase of a phenomenon that historians call the Great Awakening. It was what the name implies: faith that had been slumbering stirred again.

The movement was both demonic and exalted, creative and destructive. On the positive side, it led to the founding of many schools, among them Princeton, Brown, and Dartmouth. It added substantially to church membership. But it racked the Presbyterian Church, jumbled the Dutch Reformed Church, started schisms between Congregational parishes. It weakened the whole organizing principle of a Holy Commonwealth under God which had shaped the first years of colonial America.

It is ironic that this emotional explosion began with the low-keyed Edwards. As a preacher he never used inflammatory tricks, but the cumulative impact of his quiet passion in the pulpit happened to juxtapose with the shaking effect on the community of the sudden deaths of two of its young people in 1734. In that charged atmosphere Edwards preached a series of powerful expository sermons on the chapter about love in I Corinthians (ch. 13). Next, the only general store in town burned down. Its owner, Deacon Ebenezer Hunt, suffered heavy losses, so neighbors collected for him a handsome sum for the times: £50. Two local ne'er-do-wells announced that they were converted. The young people in town, accustomed to meet for parties after church on Sunday evenings, began holding prayer groups instead. By December of 1734 when a young woman who had been a famous flirt said that God had "given her a new heart," Edwards reported that "Religion was the one topic of conversation . . . scarcely a single person in the whole town was left unconcerned about the great things of the eternal world." *

Realizing the danger of hysteria, Edwards tried to channel his people's ardor into singing meetings which he hoped might burn off some of the emotionalism. He drew up a guide to test a person's depth of conviction, entitling it "Directions for Judging of a Person's Experiences." He counseled constantly with individuals, trying to show them how to use conversion as a first step in a sensible plan for their lives. He stressed that sincere actions were more convincing witness to one's faith than dramatic gestures. But a fury had been unleashed.

More than 550 people, half of them men, joined the church. The parsonage buzzed with visitors. People from other towns came to see the excitement. "Sight-seers came scornfully and seemed not to know what to make of it," said Edwards. When the district court convened in March, many who came to town for those sessions stopped in to see what was going on in the church. The Thursday-night meetings drew visitors from as far away as Groton, Connecticut, down on the shore. The move-

---

* A pleasant milestone was passed that same year. Since Indian raids were unlikely, the town common was not needed as a shelter for cows. So the grazing of cows on the town green was prohibited, and the plot became an attractive park in the center of the village.

ment spread to South Hadley, Hatfield, Deerfield, Long-meadow, Northfield, in Massachusetts, and down to Suffield, Connecticut, where the local preacher had the memorable name of Ebenezer Devotion.

Though she had four little girls to claim her attention, and much more company than usual to entertain, Sarah drew upon her deep inner reserves and managed to make this impression upon Hopkins:

> In the midst of these complicated labours . . . [Edwards] found at home one who was in every sense a help mate for him, one who made their common dwelling the abode of order and neatness, of peace and comfort, of harmony and love, to all its inmates, and of kindness and hospitality to the friend, the visitant, and the stranger.

For a while the revival had a bracing effect. Edwards noted that "people soon had done with their old quarrels, backbitings and intermeddling with other men's matters, the tavern was soon left empty. . . . The minister's house . . . was thronged far more than ever the tavern had been wont to be." (He lost the tavern keepers' votes right there.)

Then began an unhealthy aftermath. People could not sleep, for they were brought "to the borders of despair . . . a terrifying sense of God's anger." Edwards battled to keep the movement sensible. "A great deal of caution and pains were found necessary to keep the people, many of them, from running wild." Hoping to temper the excesses, he drew up a hardheaded covenant with specific promises about how the people might put their faith into actions. Then he had all the people agree to the covenant in a solemn ceremony.

The story of the revival he reported in A Faithful Narrative of the Surprising Work of God . . . in Northampton. Originally this had been a personal letter to Dr. Benjamin Colman, minister in Cambridge. Colman thought the account was so interesting that he shared it with Thomas Prince and Prince's associate minister, Dr. Sewall. The Boston clergy sent it along to England with an enthusiastic preface. There it was heartily received. One minister panted, "Never did we hear or read, since the first ages of Christianity, any event of this kind so surprising." The famous English hymn writer, Isaac Watts, wrote the preface to the English edition of the report, saying, "This thing was not done in a corner." When John Wesley read it on a walk from London to Oxford in 1738, he exclaimed, "Surely this is the Lord's doing and it is marvellous in our eyes."

But by then the barometer had dropped in Northampton. In 1735 a terrifying epidemic of sore throat had raged through the valley. In one town ninety-nine persons died, eighty-one of them children. Again, Sarah's good fortune with her children was in contrast to the sorrow in many households. It may in part have been the result of her good sense about hygiene and the sturdiness of her brood. At any rate, her house was one of the few to be spared.

Next, the town suffered a sudden spooky invasion of crows, who filled the air with their strident gossip and woke people early with their conferences on rooftops. This added to the general edginess, and the town put a bounty on crow corpses to discourage these rasping intruders. Edwards conceded: "In the latter part of May it began to be very sensible that the Spirit of God was gradually withdrawing from us and after this time Satan seemed to be more let loose and raged in a dreadful manner."

One day Thomas Stebbins committed suicide, and then an eminent man of the community, Joseph Hawley, Sr., cut his own throat. The poet Robert Lowell, trying to insert himself into the mind of Edwards, has reflected on this gruesome scenario:

> At Jehovah's nod
> Satan seemed more let loose amongst us: God
> Abandoned us to Satan, and he pressed
> Us hard, until we thought we could not rest
> Till we had done with life. Content was gone.
> All the good work was quashed. We were undone.

> The breath of God had carried out a planned
> And sensible withdrawal from this land;
> The multitude, once unconcerned with doubt,
> Once neither callous, curious nor devout,
> Jumped at broad noon.

Periods of letdown make a man doubt the reality of God even more than he does in moments of high tragedy. Aftermaths . . . the morning after a daughter is married; a college campus on the evening of commencement; a convention hall after a candidate has been nominated and the used coffee cups and parade placards remain . . . these are scenes that test us with jaded spirits. Such was the mood of Northampton as the first phase of the Awakening receded.

The weather that winter was sensationally cold—the kind of chill that tenses the muscles and stiffens the nostrils. Wood was burned as fast as it could be carried into the kitchen, and Sarah had a baby to keep clean. No one but her husband had a hint that it was happening, but Sarah now entered a period of darkness. Others were not aware that demons clawed her, for she had been trained to be as poised as a princess. A queen does not droop when people are looking. The Sarah who was princess-exemplar pushed herself to be perfect, but the glandular part of her got tired and irascible, was fully human.

Perhaps she became aware of her inner inconsistency one morning of that interminable February of 1737 after the children had been caged indoors with colds and she awoke to hear again the nasty tap of sleet on shutters. The human Sarah wanted to burrow back into a pillow. The noble Sarah forced herself to go downstairs and fry bacon for ten people. Or it could have been a spring day when apple trees were blossoming and the air whispered of wanderlust and young love while she, combing her dark hair, noticed a gray streak. Or she may have wondered suddenly when Edwards was away on a trip why a man was free to ride off while a woman stayed with a nursing baby.

It speaks of the singularity of her relationship with Edwards that she let him see what no other onlooker suspected—her human shortcomings. He later wrote about her that she "had been subject to unsteadiness and many ups and downs . . . often subject to melancholy." The rest of the world saw only the Sarah which Hopkins decribed:

> When she herself labored under bodily disorders and pains, which was not infrequently the case, instead of troubling those around her with her complaints, and wearing a sour or dejected countenance, as if out of humor with everybody and everything around her because she was disregarded and neglected; she was accustomed to bear up under them not only with patience but with cheerfulness and good humor.

Edwards wrote in retrospect that in this period his wife had "a disposition to censure and condemn others," but Hopkins was under the impression that

> she made it her rule to speak well of all, so far as she could with truth and justice to herself and others. . . . Thus she was tender of everyone's character, even of those who injured or spoke evil of her.

If there really is such a phenomenon as a saintly character, it seems often to be formed after a stage of conflict and anguish. In time even the candid Edwards was to report that after this period of torment his wife emerged with "the greatest, fullest longest continued and most constant assurance of the favor of God that I ever saw . . . in any person." But such maturity comes at a price. One hurdle Sarah still had to surmount was her need to feel popular with everyone. This was an inconvenient trait in a woman whose husband had begun to acquire active antagonists.

One was Edwards' own cousin, Chester Williams. He lived nearby, and Edwards continued to call on him, though he was snubbed. Williams subscribed to a milder variety of Calvinism called Arminianism, after Jacobus Arminius who lived in Holland from 1560 to 1609. Arminius modified the strict Calvinist ideas of predestination and original sin; and later Arminian parties went beyond this to the point of arguing that God had given men freedom to choose sin or salvation. Edwards had a complex idea that man's action is caused by everything that has made him what he is, his choices are shaped by all that has happened to him, by his entire life, past and present. Edwards argued that a man's personality is a cumulative unity and that excellency is his consent to this way in which God has chosen to bring redemption to a grubby world. He mistrusted Arminianism because he thought it could be used to manipulate virtue for man's own comfort. Such a theological dispute seems a silly reason for a family feud, but Chester Williams turned his head away when he had to ride past the Edwards house. This frayed relationship haunted Sarah.

Another enemy Edwards acquired by bad luck, not his own fault. He took seriously the responsibility for sharing in the Congregational ordering of society, so one of his priorities was the Hampshire Association of Ministers. Thus he was drawn into the matter of ordaining Robert Breck. This curious candidate for the ministry had been a gambler, a hard drinker, and suspected of stealing at Harvard. He tried to be ordained in Connecticut, but President Clap at Yale had heard about Breck's reputation and blocked him. Breck moved north to Massachusetts and tried again.

The Association asked Breck to get a letter from Clap confirming his "orthodoxy," so Breck swallowed his pride and wrote to Clap, asking "Christian forgiveness." By the time the clergy group in Massachusetts met to decide on the case, it was notorious. A noisy crowd milled around the meetinghouse to hoot at Clap when, intransigent, he rode up with his saddlebag full of damaging evidence about Breck. After the meeting was over and Clap came outside, the crowd "acted like boys let out of school." Those in the Association against ordaining Robert Breck had won by one vote. Though Edwards had not even been at that meeting, his writing talent was so esteemed that the Association persuaded him to prepare the report of the decision. The episode left a smudge on the church politics in the colony and it left Edwards with a vigorous enemy in Breck.

The foundation of the meetinghouse had become "considerably disordered" with the passage of years, so the congregation voted to build a new house of worship. There was bickering about the location, for some wanted the building moved to another site. But work had begun in the summer of 1736. A hard rain in September slowed down construction and the people were still meeting in the old building through the winter. The cruel cold spell had been followed by a crazy early spring, with a sudden thaw. One Sunday in March of 1737 an astonishing accident occurred while the people were gathered for worship. As Edwards reported: "In the midst of the public exercise . . . soon after the beginning of the sermon . . . the whole gallery-full of people—suddenly and without any warning—sunk and fell down, with the most amazing noise upon the heads of those that sat under. . . . The falling gallery seemed to be broken all to pieces . . . so that some who fell with it, as well as those who were under were buried in the ruins; and were found pressed under heavy loads of timber . . . but every life [was] preserved. . . . There is not . . . a bone broken or so much as put out of joint." March, the most malevolent month in the New England year, was predictably Edwards' unlucky month. It was to be the time when his health and his judgment touched their nadir. This weird accident was a portent.

That spring the town hummed with building noises, for in addition to the construction on the meetinghouse carpenters were hard at work on a new courthouse. The church officials were occupied by the touchy matter of who was to sit where. (That was still an issue in 1782 in New Haven when a tutor's wife started an argument by claiming that she outranked a president's daughter.) Elihu Parsons, Col. John Stoddard, Colonel Dwight, and Seth Pomeroy toiled for hours over the seating charts. One person even dared to suggest that husbands be allowed to sit with wives, but this novel proposal was voted down. Finally, the harassed committee worked out a plan whereby Colonel Stoddard and Joseph Hawley, Jr., sat in the most prestigious seats, just beyond Sarah. The middle-sized children of the parish, including the Edwardses' daughter Sarah, were in the second row, with deacons sprinkled strategically in their midst to discourage any shenanigans. The new building held 738 people and had three entrances, with a small porch on the west end. There were six persons to a pew on the ground floor, but in the humble gallery pews nine people had to squeeze into a row.

A move into a new church building is an electric event for the people who have worked hard to achieve it. The Edwards children had checked in with the carpenters each day, to enjoy the shouts and hammering and to study the progress of the construction. Their parents had lived through every jot of the calculations of design and finances. Then came the day of fulfillment when hope was as unscuffed as freshly painted doorsteps. Edwards climbed for the first time into the high pulpit where his encounter with the Transcendent would transform boards and paint, bell rope and Bible, into the house of God.

In July while Joseph Bellamy was a guest in the house, breakfast was unusually disorganized because Sarah was busy having a baby. At last it was a son, Timothy. He became a sober child, unlike his effervescent sisters. Timothy was to be a probate judge, a colonel in the Revolution, a solid citizen but not a joyous one. One reason why this boy did not turn out to be as blithe as the girls may have been that in the first years of his life, when a child is most affected by his mother, Sarah was emotionally erratic. She went on functioning as if nothing was wrong. To the outside observer she still appeared almost superhumanly sweet. Hopkins again: "She took almost the whole direction of the temporal affairs of the family, without doors and within, managing them with great wisdom and prudence, as well as cheerfulness."

Sarah wasn't chewed by the aspirations that make a modern

woman restless. A different climate of expectation surrounded a woman then. Not even an educated and privileged one like Sarah imagined any role that might compete with a man. But in this period of physical depletion after childbirth, her disproportionate responsibilities began to overtax her.

The sharpest sorrow is the one we dare not confide to any other. A death or obvious disaster is at least evident to others, and friends can comfort us with casseroles and kindly notes. But the shadow we must carry in secret forces us to listen to admonitions about why we should perk up. We must maintain the facade of poise when we really want to screech: "My husband is having an affair . . . My son has become a surly stranger . . . I love to distraction someone I dare not even name . . . I'm afraid my daughter is beginning to steal things . . . Today is my birthday—and where has my life gone?" So for Sarah the hardest aspect of the emotional season she had entered may have been that she could not articulate it. She could not even allow herself to think: I'm not as endlessly giving as I appear to be, and this is an impossibly difficult man. So she stuffed the lid back on the box of snakes and continued to pour tea charmingly.

But Edwards noticed that there were shadows under her eyes and that at night, unguarded in sleep, she sighed. He persuaded her to leave the children and take a trip to Boston with him.

William Hogg, a Scot whom they had never met, decided that he wanted to know what his correspondents looked like. When Hogg heard that a young British artist, Joseph Badger, was going to Boston, he commissioned Badger to do portraits of Sarah and Jonathan, and also sent money for the cost of the journey. So Sarah had a fine reason to take a holiday alone with her husband.

Travel by horseback is a form of travel like sailing—it links man and nature, and allows for leisure to look at beauty. The Edwardses followed a road that had first been tramped by Indians carrying corn between Boston and the Connecticut

Valley. It had been designated a colonial highway in 1673, and led to Boston through gentle terrain where it was possible to cover as much as thirty miles a day, except on hills and at streams that had to be forded. At noon they dismounted and stretched while the horses grazed. At night they stopped with the handiest parson, as many had stopped with them.

On the third day they clattered up a hill overlooking the rich, young, busy city of Boston. In 1740, Boston pulsated. Its symbol was a forest of ship masts in its harbor, for the invention of the Yankee Schooner in 1713 by Capt. Andrew Robinson had brought faster travel, and a boom in commerce. Masts were the product that linked the great American forests with the ocean, tied the New England colonies to the rest of the world. A good mast 100 feet high could bring as much as £90 sterling on the market after it had been cut in deep snow, dragged behind oxen from a forest, then floated down a river to a shipyard. It was new America's most characteristic product.

About the wharf was a tangle of sloops, schooners, whalers, and fishing ketches. One thousand ships a year put out of Boston, and the city smelled of fish and marlin. Sedan chairs and brightly painted wagons of red, yellow, and blue added to the colorfulness of the street scenes. So did the signs of taverns and shops, some of them painted by such expert artists as the famed Benjamin West. The city was jostling, confident, gaudy, a planet removed from the quiet hayfields of Northampton.

For Jonathan, Boston meant a chance to graze in bookstores such as the Heart and Crown on Cornhill. For Sarah, it was a chance to catch up on fashions. She had many daughters to dress and she had kept her New Haven feeling for elegance. So she peered in shop windows where baby dolls displayed samples of the London styles. Later, keeping that picture in her head, she would add lace to the sleeves of last year's dress to make it look new, would revive another with a new white apron.

Many women in that day had aged by the time they were as old as Sarah. They quickly ran out of calcium, and thought "a tooth for every child" was an inexorable rule of nature. Hair fell out and bodies sagged. But Sarah's husband made it clear that he treasured her as more than a housekeeping drudge and the mother of extra farmhands. So she stayed attractive, and fifteen years later she was still able to entrance men much younger than she was. For such a woman, a shopping trip to a city like Boston was as reviving as the return of April. For both Edwardses, the best part of the holiday was a chance to see friends with whom they did not need to explain themselves or deprecate their learning. The trip gave both of them a reprieve from the pressures of Northampton.

As for the picture that was painted, Hogg gave the portraits to John Erskine and after Edwards' death Jonathan, Jr., tried to purchase them. Erskine insisted on making him a gift of them, and the portraits passed down through the family until a descendant of the couple, J. Walter Edwards, of Bridgehampton, New York, had to make a decision. As he explained it, "My cousin Eugene Phelps Edwards of Stonington . . . had made a will bequeathing the portraits to [me]. He wrote to me saying that the portraits should rightfully come to me but raising the question of whether they should go to Yale where they would receive expert care. I replied, in what is the only unselfish act of my life, that I thought he should leave them to Yale, which he did."

Sarah was to draw heavily upon the inner resources she had been able to accumulate on the trip in the year that followed. On June 20 she had another baby, Susanna, whom everyone was to call "Sukey," and after her confinement melancholy was added to her weariness. Her sister Mary was married to William Russell, minister of the church in Middletown, Connecticut, a trading port and at that time the wealthiest community in the state. Mary was only thirty-eight years old, but she died on June 24, just after Sukey had arrived. The death of a brother or sister strikes at the very center of us, for it begins the chipping away of the world we know. So the death of Mary Russell shook Sarah.

Then in October of that year there whirled into Northampton a visitor so unusual that he took everyone's mind off
previous agendas. The visitor who left a colorful mark on his
era was himself strongly affected by Sarah Edwards.

George Whitefield was an English evangelist who was famous
on both sides of the ocean. He had made thirteen Atlantic
crossings at a time when ocean voyages were not pleasure
cruises. He may have been a prophet, or a buffoon, or possibly
a blend of both. His voice was fantastic. Benjamin Franklin
once stood half a mile away in a crowd he estimated to be
thirty thousand and he claimed that he heard Whitefield well.
The skeptical Franklin for some reason took a shine to Whitefield, and invited him to lodge above his press shop. He printed
his sermons, helped raise funds to build an auditorium for him.
Many of the dandified society were charmed by him. The
Virginia Gazette of August 24, 1739, said:

> Several fine ladies who used to wear French silks, French
> hoops of 4 yards wide, Tete de Mouton Heads [wigs]
> . . . and white Satin Smock-Petticoats and c. are turned
> Methodists and Followers of Mr. Whitefield. . . . They
> now wear plain Stuff Gowns, no Hoops.

Not everyone found him enchanting. Dr. Johnson growled:
"His popularity, sir, is chiefly owing to the peculiarity of his
manner. He would be followed by crowds were he to wear
a nightcap in the pulpit or were he to preach from a tree."
Horace Walpole lampooned Whitefield's charities:

> Drop, to atone, your money at the door,
> And if I please—I'll give it to the poor.

Charles Chauncy wrote to George Wishart of Edinburgh:
"The grand subject of Conversation was Mr. Whitefield and
the whole Business of the Town to run, from Place to Place,
to hear him preach." Other clergy feared to lend their pulpits
to someone so sensational, so Whitefield preached in the fields,
to gigantic crowds. The actor David Garrick was fascinated by
Whitefield's dramatic talent, and said that he could make

audiences weep or tremble just by varying his pronunciation of
the word "Mesopotamia." Garrick slyly added: "His eloquence
advanced up to its 40th repetition before it reached its full
height."

The paradox of Whitefield mirrored the incongruities of the
English social scene. Religion bored Horace Walpole, the
witty letter writer who in 1741 took the seat in the House of
Commons which he was to hold with distinction for thirty-six
years. The gamy paintings of Hogarth satirized pious hypocrisy.
Yet while British opinion makers ridiculed religion, new sects
were sprouting all over the Islands. (That was when the French
began to quip that the English were a people of one hundred
religions and only one sauce.) Whitefield was a resounding
success in England and his trip to America in 1740 and 1741
ignited a second phase of the Awakening.

Whitefield was capable of rather touching self-insight, as in
this entry in his *Journal:* "Alas, Alas. In how many things have
I judged and acted wrong. . . . Being fond of scripture language, I have used a style too apostolical and at the same time
I have been too bitter in my zeal. Wild-fire has been mixed
with it, and I find that I frequently wrote and spoke in my own
spirit, when I thought I was writing and speaking by the
assistance of the spirit of God." He could also show a nice
sense of humor, as in his reminiscence about reforming one
terrible Scotsman who "used to swear to ease his Stomach."
Yet this same man, Whitefield, could turn about and make
a preposterous announcement such as, "I will assure you, Moses
was a Methodist." He once skirted close to slander when he
asserted, "Archbishop Tillotson knew no more about true Christianity than Mahomet." Some clergymen in New Jersey found
him unappetizing, and tried to discourage him from putting on
revival meetings in their churches. Barred from one pulpit,
Whitefield had four cronies lock the resident preacher in a pew
box, while Whitefield climbed into his pulpit. Of Whitefield's
tour of America in 1740, Thomas Prince remarked that "Boston
had never seen anything like it before, except at the time of

the general Earthquake." At the height of his triumph, Whitefield came to Northampton, on October 17, 1740.

In New England, where winter is stern, October catches the
heart. That fall the hills around Northampton raged with
color. The air was sweet with the smell of the apple orchards
that were a characteristic of cider-loving colonial America. The
agitated scuffling of squirrels in dry leaves said, "Hurry! Hurry!"
The eye reveled in the gorgeousness, though a passing cloud
would bring a premonitory chill. The combination of autumn's
poignant beauty and the certainty that the beauty would soon
vanish set the mood for Whitefield's visit.

He preached four times during the weekend and had one
small session in the parsonage. On Saturday morning he talked
privately with the Edwards children, who, he noted approvingly
in his *Journal*, "were dressed not in Silks and Satins, but plain."
Though Whitefield had openly been of the opinion that most
ministers were "wolves in sheeps' cloathing," he liked Edwards. "I think, I may say I have not seen his Fellow in all
New England." He was most impressed by Sarah, to a point
where he wrote:

"A sweeter Couple I have not yet seen. . . . She . . . talked
feelingly and solidly of the Things of God, and seemed to be
such a Help meet for her Husband that she caused me to . . .
[pray] God, that he would be pleased to send me a Daughter
of *Abraham* to be my wife." This was an astonishing observation from Whitefield, a bachelor so prissy that someone had
remarked, "He did not think he should die easy if he thought
his gloves were out of place." But after his exposure to Sarah
Edwards, Whitefield went out wife-hunting for himself. The
next year he married a widow ten years older than he, but one
whom Wesley described as a "woman of candour and humanity."

The winter of 1740 and 1741 turned out to justify any appre-
hensions felt in October, for it was the most severe anyone
could remember. Men drove horses and carriages on ice-covered
Long Island Sound. Down in Philadelphia the Quaker John

Woolman told how the Delaware River was frozen from December 15 through March, and market was conducted halfway between its shores. Many sheep and cattle died. There was another epidemic of the dread disease Jonathan Dickinson, later to be the first president of the College of New Jersey, wrote up as "Observations of that Terrible Disease, vulgarly called Throat Distemper."

In the spring of 1741 there was "great uneasiness" in town because Edwards asked for a clear salary understanding. This was a radical request. Most ministers supplemented their income with erratic gifts and handouts. Ezra Stiles received in one year: a cow, a calf, a milking pail, a load of hay, a velvet cloak for his wife, a coat for himself, a cradle for his baby, a cheese, a turkey, a side of beef, a bridle—all as fringe benefits. He also picked up some profits by investing in sea voyages by his parishioners. In 1763, Stiles shipped out 15 gallons of rum and received on the return trip a profitable 769 pounds of Carolina rice. The first salmon caught each year in Newbury, Massachusetts, traditionally went to the minister. Boston's diarist Judge Samuel Sewall once wrote that he had called on the preacher and "carried him a bushel of Turnips, cost me 5 shillings, and a cabbage cost half a crown."

Funerals were a prime source of extra income. Many ministers received as funeral favors a white scarf, to be worn folded over the right shoulder. A wife who was a handy seamstress found many ways to use these scarves. When Sarah Van Brugh died in 1742 in New York, her family economized by giving out linen rather than silk scarves, yet they still had a bill of £500 for funeral favors. A popular minister also was given many gloves at funerals. Andrew Eliot of Old North Church in Boston left such a collection of kidskin and lamb's-wool gloves that when they were bartered in 1742, they brought the equivalent of $640. Other ministers received mourning rings—small gold bands similar to wedding rings. Dr. Sam Buxton, of Salem, left a tankard of them when he died in 1758. Perhaps the champion at acquiring fringe benefits was Anthony Stoddard. For sixty years minister in Woodbury, Connecticut, he was also clerk of the probate clerk and town doctor. The town gave him a fine house and a maximum land allotment—and the house was his own. He left an estate of £1,000 in 1760.

Many towns gave a minister a chance to enchance his salary by tutoring boys for college or by doing bleedings. But Edwards was not a man with a talent for fawning on people who might reward him with gifts or perquisites.

An argument about ministers' salaries had been building up in many towns. In 1706 an anonymous "friend to the churches" published A Plea for the Ministers of the Gospel. The gist of it was that the clergy's prestige would decline unless they were paid at least as much as merchants or tradesmen. In 1725 another anonymous pamphlet, Anti-Ministerial Objections Considered claimed that many towns thought "a cheap minister is the Best." It argued that if clergy were still to lead the community, they must be more than "middling livers." This debate came at a sensitive time, when the American economy was unstable. No settled form of currency had been worked out for the colonies, and barter was a common form of commerce.

Part of the trouble came from honest misunderstanding about the nature of work. Few people comprehended that a man may be working very hard when he is thinking. On the frontier, most men worked prodigiously with their muscles. Plows were heavy, and so were the blacksmiths' hammers and the axes that whacked down masts for ships. Pounding flax in the hot days of late June was a backbreaking chore. Parishioners with aching muscles and calloused hands resented a soft-handed clergyman whose tool was a pen. The scorn of the busy layman for the sedentary parson was expressed in 1753 by lawyer William Livingston, who described "a little airy coxcomb, too lazy to work and too proud to beg . . . [who] jumps into commission with a Lye in his Mouth that he is moved by the Holy Ghost, when his highest Aim is a fat living."

It had been different in Stoddard's time. In the early years of the colonies, the leadership of a learned clergy was vital.

Moreover, Stoddard had independent wealth. (His many children had diminished the estate, however, and none of it was coming to Edwards). No one whispered when Stoddard ate from fine china, though other people had wooden bowls. He had the only gold watch in town and was the first to drink tea. Even Judge Sewall, who had been niggardly about his local clergyman, freely heaped gifts on Stoddard. He always sent back for Madame Stoddard a piece of "commencement cake," or two-pound sacks of raisins and almonds, or large chunks of chocolate when her husband came to Harvard functions. But Stoddard was a different sort of man, and that had been a very different era. His place had never been questioned.

When Edwards came to the church, he received ten acres of pasture, forty acres of meadow and ten additional acres on a hill, as well as £300 toward his house and £100 a year as salary. This was a handsome amount for a country preacher then. In 1731, after babies began to appear, he was given £40 more, then £100 was added the next year. Each increase jangled nerves in the town.

There was more to the situation. A mood that was to produce the Revolution was also showing in revolt against such autocratic clergy as the notorious man who said, "I do not serve my parish, I rule it." One way parishes expressed their displeasure in a preacher was to forget to stock his wood supply. One chilly November Sunday the Reverend Mr. French of Andover, Massachusetts, wryly announced, "I will write two discourses and deliver them in this meeting house on Thanksgiving Day, provided I can manage to write them without a fire."

The *Boston News Letter* of November 18, 1728, printed a sample budget for eight persons in "Families of Middling Figure who bear the Character of being Genteel." It allowed for beer, for soap for baths once in four weeks, for three candles a night, for a maid at £10 a year, and three pairs of shoes each year. The Edwardses fitted this bracket, yet the sample budget made no provision for the entertaining Sarah did incessantly, for charitable gifts, for letter-writing, or for schooling. All of these were necessities of life for the Edwardses.

Sharp eyes scrutinized the clothes Sarah and the girls wore to church. In the valley, there was a long tradition of regarding fancy clothes with suspicion. People who had less than £200 in property were prohibited by law from wearing silver or gold buttons. Ladies were frowned on for appearing in public with a knot of ribbon at the shoulder. A Northampton court had tried Hannah Lyman, aged sixteen, for "wearing silk in a flaunting manner." So the town watched for signs of extravagance in the ladies of the Edwards household. They also whispered about the fact that Edwards himself had his suits tailored in Boston.

Dr. Mather, at Edwards' request, was put on a committee to discuss salary with him. Mather tried to be reconciling, but the other members of the committee rammed through a humiliating ruling that Sarah had to keep an itemized statement of parsonage expenses. Later, Sarah recalled:

> I remember Mr. Edwards once said . . . the difficulties he had a Prospect of appeared to Him like a Bottomless ocean, he could see no end of 'em. I once asked Him whether it was worth his while to strive to have his salary settled seeing He thought it probable this difficulty would end in a separation between Him and his people. He answered, there were so great difficulties arose through the salary being unsettled that though he tarried but a year or two he chose to have it done.

One other event stood out, in the year 1741. In June, Edwards had preached in his own church with no effect a sermon entitled "Sinners in the Hands of an Angry God." His own parishioners had listened lethargically and then, unscathed by the sermon, had strolled outdoors to talk about whether the sunshine would hold up for the haying season. But on July 8, Edwards attended a conference in Enfield, Connecticut, and was asked on short notice to preach there. He dipped into his saddlebag and hauled out the sermon he had preached to his own congregation without causing a ripple of reaction.

In the plain little country church of Enfield he made homi-
letic history. People "yelled and shrieked, they rolled in the
aisles, they crowded up into the pulpit and begged him to
stop." One observer reported: "One waited with the deepest
and most solemn solicitude to hear the trumpet sound . . .
and was deeply disappointed when the day terminated and left
the world in its usual state of tranquility."

Henry Ward Beecher later commented, "I think a person
of moral sensibilities, alone at midnight, reading that awful
discourse, would well-nigh go crazy." The people in Enfield
that Sunday were in an expectant mood to hear the visiting
preacher who was said to be famous even across the Atlantic
Ocean. They did not take him for granted as Edwards' home
church did. They did not hear him all the time, so they listened
with fresh sensibilities. What he said slashed through to the
hearers as a sermon seldom has in all of history.

The second phase of the Awakening crested in the spring
and summer of 1741. Edwards believed that it had produced
"a remarkable and general alteration in the face of New England." At least 10 percent of New England's population claimed
to be converted. Instead of exulting in these statistics, Edwards
was saddened by a mood he sensed. He who cherished orderly
continuity in society saw the revival movement splintering
churches now. He who tried to be rational saw the religious
experience grotesquely distorted by emotionalism.

Two men were most responsible for the new mood. One was
James Davenport, a revivalist who was in fact teetering on the
edge of sanity. He had been storming into Connecticut parson-
ages, quizzing the preacher, then leaving with the verdict that
the minister was not a man of God. Later, Davenport wrote
a moving public apology: "I had the long fever on me and
the cankry humour raging at once . . . though I thought, in
the time of it, that 't was the Spirit of God in high degree."
He went back to call on one minister he had insulted and the
man said, "He came with such a meek, mild, pleasant and
humble spirit, broken and contrite as I scarce ever saw."

Davenport ended by settling down as a respectable Presbyterian clergyman in New Jersey.

The other disturber of the peace was Gilbert Tennent, minister of the Presbyterian Church in New Brunswick, New Jersey. Tennent had introduced there "a method of close personal preaching coupled with intensive and searching counseling." In 1735, coinciding with the revival in Northampton, Tennent published four of his innovative sermons and an account of his methods of conversion. Some of his colleagues in the Synod of New Jersey parted from his contention that the power of a minister's labors came not from his personal holiness but from "God's call" to him. This led to a rift in 1741 over whether vacant pulpits should be filled by men approved by the official church governing body or by preachers who simply announced that they were appointed by God. The schism lasted seventeen years and eventually was healed by Tennent's own growth in magnanimity. He later apologized for the "excessive heat of temper" he had shown. It was in part the result of his grief over the death of his wife—he described it as a time of "great spiritual desertion." In 1758, Tennent presided over the reuniting meeting which brought back together the splintered synods, but in 1742 he was a problem for Edwards. He was going about New England conducting revival meetings almost as hectic as those of Davenport.

The spectacle prompted one friend of Edwards to write to Bellamy: "There are some things that persons are apt to run into at the present day that we ought not to encourage . . . taking their own passions and imaginations for the operations of God's spirit, giving heed to visions, trances and revelations." These were Edwards' own reservations about the methods of Gilbert Tennent and James Davenport.

Against this background, Edwards was given a hard assignment. He was asked to be speaker at the Yale commencement in September, 1741. Of all those who disapproved of emotionalism, one of the most hostile critics was Thomas Clap, Yale's president. Everyone waited to hear whether Edwards

would repudiate the excesses that had been carried on in the
name of religion. Everyone watched the face of President Clap as
he listened to the speaker. Edwards tried to use this opportunity
to bring the Awakening under rational control again. His
sermon was called "The Distinguishing Marks of a Work of
the Spirit of God" and in its clean, carefully crafted sentences
it analyzed the revival, concluding that it was "in general from
the Spirit of God." Davenport and Tennent were delighted by
this, though Edwards had said: "They who leave the sure word
of prophecy . . . to follow such impressions and impulses,
leave the polar star to follow a Jack-with-a-lantern."

The Yale commencement was a carnival that night, with all
the windows on New Haven green lighted by candles. There
were fireworks and many flowing punchbowls. At Harvard
during that period, commencements were toasted so enthusiastically that one jingle said:

> "Thus the loose Croud forbidden Pleasures seek,
> Drink Harvard dry, and so conclude the week."

But President Clap made it clear that he was not in a festive
mood, and the evening was dismal for Edwards. Then he
journeyed home to face a crisis in the life of his wife.

# VIII

## To the Breaking Point and Back

To see in the "eternal feminine's" ideal of passivity and self-containment the seeds of self-paralysis and self-alienation is the great task of the modern era, resembling that task already recognized to establish, through love, the authentic self of the infant.

—*Dan Sullivan*

We wish we could erase the whole month of January, 1742. But because this episode in the life of Sarah Edwards was so peculiar, so unlike the character she showed in all the rest of her years, it is inescapable.

Here we don't like her at all. The serene mother becomes limply needful. The patient wife comes to the end of her patience. The attractive hostess becomes grotesque—jabbering, hallucinating, idiotically fainting. We are embarrassed for her. But isn't this what each of us does in our bad dreams? what sometimes we refrain from doing by the thinnest edge of self-control? what we finally do when we have a nervous breakdown?

Here Sarah stands exposed as a fully human woman. One with a breaking point as any woman has. Before, she *had* been too good to be true.

But, and here is mystery, this blackness was over soon and she never went through such an episode again. We would prefer to dodge this awkward spot, but it is the heart of her story. Such a period of anguish seems to be often the necessary step before a person fully feels the transforming power of God. This was Jacob's night of wrestling with the angel, Benedict's roll in the rosebush, the mythic struggle.

Neither is there any explanation for the peace that comes on the far side of such confusion. Jacob was blessed by the angel as dawn broke. Benedict went on to preserve the life of the intellect through the Dark Ages. Sarah went back to her routine, more efficient than before. But for one month in 1742, as snow sparkled on the Hampshire hills, Sarah Edwards went to pieces.

For the first fourteen years of the marriage of Sarah and Jonathan Edwards, she seemed to the outside world to be the sunny and stable member of the team. While Edwards pampered his headaches and his finicky colon, she would scarcely pause when she shucked off a baby. Hopkins reports of her:

> She was unmindful of any pain or affliction. . . . As he was of a weakly, infirm constitution . . . she was a tender nurse to him, cheerfully attending upon him at all times, and in all things ministering to his comfort.

The wife expected to be Spartan in those days. One woman wrote in her diary: "Took Physic and consulted the physician, all to no purpose. Suspected the disorder to be nervous, faced about, put on great resolution and made mince pies and found myself no worse than before."

The casual observer saw the difficult husband, the endlessly giving wife. Actually, more than anyone on the outside guessed, *she* leaned on *him*. Though she carried all the practical details of managing the house, Sarah depended on Edwards for her own spiritual replenishment. She would dart into his study during the day, confident that no matter how intent he was on his writing, he would put down his pen and turn to her with lighted face. She fed on his leadership of family prayers and on the quiet time she and Edwards spent together on devotions after the children were in bed, the time that put a benediction on all the bustle of the daylight hours. When

Edwards was away, she had to carry all the complex administration of a large household without nourishment for her own inner self, without someone she could allow to share her fears and failings. She could take anything but his absences.

Edwards knew this and he worried about the mounting calls upon him to travel. He confided to Bellamy on January 21, 1742; "I desire your Prayers that God would quicken and Revive us again and particularly that he would greatly humble and pardon and quicken me." He went on to turn down an invitation to speak in Connecticut, with this explanation: "I have lately been so much gone from my People and don't know but I must be obliged to leave 'em again next week for a fortnight, being called to Leicester, a town about halfway to Boston . . . and probably soon after that to another place, and having at this Time some Extraordinary affairs to attend to at Home."

These were the "Extraordinary affairs" he mentioned: On January 19, as Sarah described herself,

> I felt very uneasy and unhappy. . . . I thought I very much needed help from God. . . . I had for some time been earnestly wrestling with God. . . . I felt within myself great quietness of spirit, unusual . . . willingness to wait upon him, with respect to the time and manner in which he should help me, and wished that he should take his own time and his own way to do it.

In spite of this protestation about her patience with God, her nerves were actually stretched like an overtuned viola, so that she was crushed when, the next morning, Edwards mildly pointed out to her that she might have been tactless in a conversation she had had the previous day with "Mr. Williams of Hadley." (This was probably the same relative who had been huffy since the first days of the Awakening, and had since snubbed every irenic gesture from the Edwardses. This deteriorated relationship had increasingly` bothered Sarah.) When Edwards suggested that she might have handled Williams more adroitly, she crumbled.

> I found that it seemed to bereave me of the quietness
> and calm of my mind, in any respect not to have the good
> opinion of my husband. This I much disliked in myself.

She goes on to explain:

> The peace and calm of my mind . . . seemed sensibly
> above the reach of disturbance from anything but these
> two: 1st my own good name and fair reputation among
> men, and especially the esteem and just treatment of the
> people of this town; 2dly And, more especially, the esteem
> and love and kind treatment of my husband.

So Edwards, in his casual remark about her handling of the
difficult Mr. Williams, punctured Sarah's two most vulnerable
points—her anxiety about offending people and her need to be
approved by her husband. Edwards had not been able to extricate himself from the date in Leicester, so he took off the next
day, and her first anxiety swept over Sarah.

It is curious that a minister's wife feels she has to be popular
in a parish. If a man does his work as well as he is able, his
own conscience should provide a measure of his success. Yet
almost all ministers' wives appear to need assurance that they,
too, are accepted warmly by the people. This illogical human
need was now nibbling at Sarah Edwards.

A young man named Buell had come to fill the pulpit while
Edwards was absent. Sarah says of him:

> I heard that Mr. Buell was coming to this town, and
> from what I had heard of him and of his success, I had
> strong hopes that there would be great effects from his
> labors here. At the same time . . . it greatly concerned
> me to watch my heart and see to it that I was perfectly
> resigned to God, with respect to the instruments he should
> make use of to revive religion in this town, and be entirely
> willing, if it was God's pleasure, that he should make use
> of Mr. Buell.

This, being translated, may have meant that she was afraid the
people might like Mr. Buell better than they liked her husband,
and that she disliked herself for feeling that way.

Often an older minister has plugged along and then had an attractive assistant whiz in, full of youthful energy and ambition. The older man may rejoice that his young associate can reach certain people who had not been touched before, but only a rare minister is not threatened. After the muted Edwards, the people of the congregation enjoyed the masculine vitality of young Buell. Edwards, on his part, had no competitiveness in his makeup. He was simply delighted by anyone of ability who could add to the work of the Kingdom. However, Edwards had always been impervious to social nuances. Sarah, whose genius was her ability to tune in on the feelings of other people, was on the other hand exceptionally vulnerable to hostility. The threat of Buell almost undid her before she was freed of jealousy forever.

President Clap at Yale had disapproved of Buell because he had appointed himself evangelist and gone riding around Connecticut in a revival team with Eleazar Wheelock, afterward founder of Dartmouth College. Buell later admitted that he had been guilty of "some imprudence and indecent heats." He said this before the Fairfield Association of Clergy, when he was asking them to ordain him. The older clergy thought Buell needed some tempering before he could qualify for ordination, so they sent him to study under Edwards. He promptly captivated the congregation, and Sarah was confronted by the need to take into her household a guest who was more popular than her husband was.

A wife who is sensitive to social opinions feels them most sharply during a minister's absence from the parish. As a single tree on a hillside is likely to draw lightning, so the minister in a Puritan community was a lone oak, a large target for speculation, gossip, and misinterpretation. When Edwards was around, he absorbed these pressures, partly because of his God-centered serenity, and partly because he was so absentminded that he did not pick up the vibrations in the community. When he was away, Sarah picked them up alone. She saw a stout old lady, whom Edwards never coddled, purring as she told Mr.

Buell about herself. And why had that knot of people lowered
their voices as Sarah walked toward the church porch? Old
Mrs. Hawley, teacup and knitting in her bag, was turning up
a neighbor's path, for an afternoon chat. What would they
talk about? With Edwards away, Sarah had no one to absorb
her fears. When she could take them to her husband, he
helped her see the smallness of the world of Northampton in
perspective against the vast sweep of the starry skies; against the
infinite mysteries of the atom; and against the other cities and
countries where the Edwards name was becoming known with
increasing respect. He cared about the little world of their
parish, but he saw it in relation to the rest of God's world.
Without Edwards near to steady her, Sarah cracked.

The beady eye of the modern psychiatrist might spot the
phase she entered as a manic one. She thought she was passing
through a period of religious ecstasy.

> On Wednesday morning . . . I sat still in entire re-
> signedness to God and willingness that God should bless
> his [Buell's] labors here as much as he pleased. . . . I
> rejoiced when I saw the honor which God put upon
> him, and the respect paid him by the people, and the
> greater success attending his preaching than had followed
> the preaching of Mr. Edwards.

She tried to persuade herself that she really believed this
when she went in the afternoon at three o'clock to a lecture
preached by Buell.

> We remained in the meeting house about three hours,
> after the public exercises were over. During most of the
> time, my bodily strength was overcome, and the joy and
> thankfulness which were excited in my mind . . . led me
> to converse with those who were near me in a very earnest
> manner.

After this jag of compulsive talking, Sarah came home to
find Buell there, talking with five guests, including her next-

door neighbor Eleanor Dwight.* She relates that the "intenseness of my feelings again took away my bodily strength. . . . I could with difficulty refrain from rising from my seat and leaping for joy."

The next day she went on managing the household—burped babies, planned food for the extra house guests, supervised snow-shoveling, but she "engaged in the duties of my family with a sweet consciousness that God was present with me." About eleven o'clock that morning, she accidentally went into one room where Buell was talking with somebody, and she quietly fainted. Buell applied a peculiar first-aid procedure. He read aloud a hymn of Isaac Watts which "made so strong an impression on my mind and my soul was drawn so powerfully towards Christ and heaven that I leaped unconsciously from my chair."

With that, Sarah fainted again and the concerned guests put her in bed, where she "lay for a considerable time, faint with joy." By this time, the whole town was buzzing. Mrs. Samuel Phelps openly worried that Sarah would die before Edwards returned "and he should think the people had killed his wife." What young Mr. Buell thought would be interesting to know. The neighbors took turns holding the household together, while Sarah

> lay on the bed from 12 o'clock till four, being too exhausted by joy to rise and sit up; and during most of the time, my feelings prompted me to converse very earnestly with one and another of those who were present.

"Enthusiasm" is an eighteenth-century word, which was used in the sense that a person was ridiculous to the verge of insanity in his religious zeal. (Dr. Johnson defined it as "vain confidence of divine favor or communication.") The mildest description of the day Sarah spent then would be "enthusiastic." The subject of sainthood is still mysterious. Some modern observers

---

* She was later to marry General Lyman, a Revolutionary War hero.

think that all religious extremes are pathological. Back in 1902 the Harvard psychologist William James, asked to deliver the Gifford Lectures in Edinburgh, examined *The Varieties of Religious Experience*. James's method of separating true religious experience from insanity he called "pragmatism," the objective scrutiny of (1) a phenomena and (2) its result. James analyzed the reports about many people who were considered saints and isolated three factors that were present in all the stories. First, the subject went through a term of restlessness, of anguished wrestling. Then came a crisis, a vision. The aftermath was joy, peace, freedom, "a transition from tenseness, self-responsibility and worry, to equanimity, receptivity and peace." James's words precisely describe the steps through which Sarah was to pass, and her case is a large portion of James's chapter entitled "Saintliness."

What happened to Sarah Edwards during that snowy week of January, 1742, her husband believed to be a theological crisis, part of the process of her conversion, the gate through which she had to stumble before she could share the full sweetness in the universe that God rules. An observer dyed in the views of Freud and his followers could come up with a psychological explanation for the week. William James confessed that he knew no "logical" explanation for such "shiftings of inner equilibrium." He simply says: "The further limits of our being plunge, it seems to me, into an altogether other dimension of existence from the sensible and merely 'understandable' world."

However one may choose to interpret this part of her story, there is no doubt whatever that afterward Sarah Edwards emerged a changed and liberated person, one whom even her husband, previously her only critic, was to consider a saint. It was a week of emotional crisis, but its aftermath was a new life, grounded on practical reality.

Meanwhile, God worked on Sarah in his mysterious way. On January 29 she woke up trembling with an anxiety about the fact that Mr. Williams of Hadley was scheduled to speak in Northampton that day. She made herself

examine my heart whether I was willing that he . . .
should be made a greater instrument of good in the town
than Mr. Edwards. . . . I never felt such an entire empti-
ness of self-love, or any regard to any private, selfish interest of my own. It seemed to me, that I had entirely
done with "myself." I felt that the opinions of the world
concerning me were nothing.

So she pulled herself together and managed to attend the
meeting. Afterward she talked feverishly with the people near
her. She went home, tried to read a bit in the Bible, and
fainted again. For the next two days she was in a transport
which some would define as a hallucination. She imagined that
she was experiencing a rhapsodic vision:

I thought if I were surrounded by enemies who were
venting their malice and cruelty upon me . . . it would
still be impossible that I should cherish any feelings toward
them but those of love and pity.

Then her other anxiety surfaced, as she thought about her
relationship with Edwards, but she concluded that

if the feelings and conduct of my husband were to be
changed from tenderness and affection, to extreme hatred
and cruelty . . . I could so rest in God that it would not
touch my heart.

The bogey of the feud with Mr. Williams still pursued her.

Just then, Mr. W. came in and spoke with a somewhat
light, smiling air of the flourishing state of religion in
the town; which I could scarcely bear to see.

Her reply to him was to faint again.

The next day, she sat at the dinner table with her large household, and had one more spell of fainting (while Mr. Buell was
holding forth to the group). But the following day a parishioner,
Mr. Lyman, who had been on an errand in Boston, stopped by
to say that he had come through Leicester on the way back. He
brought cheerful news about the success Edwards was having

there. This braced Sarah, though she had spent a sleepless night on a purely imaginary problem: "How should I feel if our house and all our property should be burnt up?" She was not the first, or last, woman to lose a night of rest on some such borrowed trouble!

Then Edwards returned. This may have been an electric confrontation. It is instructive to note the matters on which a very articulate man chooses to be silent. Edwards wrote torrentially, but he was reticent about his own role in relation to his wife here. Perhaps he felt a measure of responsibility for her slide into unreality, for the incident which had unglued her was the time that she imagined she had irritated Edwards. ("I found that it seemed to bereave me of the quietness and calm of my mind, in any respect not to have the good opinion of my husband.") There may have been forgiveness to ask and give on both sides, and then there may have been, in a deep sense, reunion.

Next, Edwards did an amazing thing. His ability to forecast future developments was both his genius and his burden. Long before anyone had thought of psychotherapy, he anticipated it. He had Sarah sit down and tell him everything she could remember about the weeks just past. Using the shorthand system he had invented, he took down her words in full. By promptly reliving the strange weeks she had just spent, Sarah seems to have discharged the pressures of fourteen taut years. From then on, she sailed through strains that would have sent another woman into bitter seclusion or into whining invalidism with migraines or sinus.

So she went back to making jams and hemming linens, but after this time her work appears to have been done without resentment. The martyred Protestant wife is a familiar figure in the social history of the West. These ladies thought they were being self-effacing when actually they were boiling beneath the surface. A surprising example of this was the wife of Bronson Alcott. The woman who was the original of the seraphic Marmee of Louisa May Alcott's Little Women once burst out:

A woman . . . lives neglected and dies forgotten . . .
but a man who never performs in his whole life one self-
denying act, but who has accidental gifts of genius, is
celebrated by his contemporaries while his name and his
works live on from age to age.

Sarah Edwards stopped straining to please God and began to
live in the assurance of a salvation she didn't have to try to
deserve. She stopped pushing herself to be worthy of Edwards'
love and from then on had his unreserved admiration. Before,
onlookers had considered her a saint but her husband knew
she wasn't. Afterward, Edwards marveled at her "constant
sweet peace, calm and serenity of soul."

William James, when he was puzzling about whether sainthood was a form of insanity, finally concluded:

By their fruits ye shall know them. The good disposition
which a vision, a voice or other apparant heavenly favor
leave behind them are the only marks by which we may be
sure they are not possible deceptions.

For the rest of their life together, Edwards was to marvel at
his wife's good disposition. As he put it, she lived with a

daily sensible doing and suffering everything for God . . .
eating for God and working for God and sleeping for God,
and bearing pain and trouble for God, and doing all as the
service of love, and so doing it with a continual, uninterrupted cheerfulness, peace and joy.

He was also struck by her

continual rejoicing in all the works of God's hands, the
works of nature, and God's daily works of providence.
[And her] wonderful access to God by prayer.

Her husband makes plain that Sarah's new sanctified state
did not make her neglect the everyday matters of actual living.
As a matter of fact, it made her more efficient, for "worldly
business has been attended with great alacrity, as part of the
service of God . . . [she has] found to be as good as prayer."

Edwards added that not only has she resumed her "relative and social duties," but showed "a noted eminence in them." On March 27, 1742, at 6:45 A.M. an earthquake made a "very loud noise" in New England. Jouncing plates and scaring babies, the physical rocking of the world matched the shaking up of Sarah Edwards.

As William James was baffled in 1902, so we still cannot be sure whether she had a religious transport, or a nervous breakdown, or whether the two were mingled. But the evidence is clear that after whatever it was, Sarah picked up life again, and went on as before, but in a new dimension of joy. Her own words may explain it. She said it left her with "the riches of full assurance." She recalled how, midway in that peculiar week, she woke and

> was led to reflect on God's mercy to me in giving me, for many years, a willingness to die, and after that . . . in making me willing to live.

The neurotic martyr is ready to die. The greater valor is to be willing to live. Her husband explained:

> Now if such things are enthusiasm and the offspring of a distempered brain; let my brain be possessed evermore of that happy distemper! If this be distraction, I pray God that the world of mankind may all be seized with this . . . glorious distraction.

And Sarah said to him, "I could sit and sing this life away."

# IX

## Rumblings

Mr. Edwards replied He must not run away.
—*Sarah Edwards*

Sarah's disturbance in the year 1742 is reflected in her one hiatus in a cycle of producing a baby every two years. There was a conspicuous pause. Then on May 8, 1743, at midnight, a daughter named Eunice arrived. Because of the new baby, Sarah was unable to accompany Edwards to clergy meetings that year, so he took along their daughter Sarah, who was then ripening into a poised young teen-ager. In September when he went down to the Yale commencement, it was their daughter Mary's turn to ride along with her father.

In New Haven, the two Edwardses met a young man named David Brainerd who was to provide the family with a later complication. The subsequent three years were uneventful, punctuated by the arrival of Jonathan, Jr., on May 26, 1745 (a Sunday). The family life turned on a quiet rhythm of worship and domesticity, planting the garden, picking the apples, studying, preparing for Sunday. It was a time of ripening, of consolidating spiritual gains, and they were to need the armor of it later.

A peripheral cloud for Sarah was concern that her family back in New Haven had caught the hostility against the Awakening. After Whitefield had visited Northampton, he had gone down to New Haven. Though the Colonial Legislature

adjourned to hear him, the university snubbed him, taking its
clue from President Clap. Sarah's brother, James Pierrepont,
chose to be allied with Whitefield. James had prospered as a
druggist in Boston and then returned to live in the family house
and be a leisured gentleman. His hobby was genealogy, and he
kept happily occupied trying to prove he was heir to the British
duke of Kingston. This would have related him to Lady Mary
Wortley Montagu, the duke's daughter and a diplomat's wife
who was herself famous as a writer of scintillating letters. This
relationship was still to be debated in the press in 1876 when
Edwards Pierrepont, American ambassador to the Court of St.
James's, claimed to have ducal ancestors. James never foresaw
that ducal wealth would come into the family line through
another source. One of his descendants was to be J. P. Morgan.

When Whitefield turned up again in New Haven in 1746,
the local clergy association advised First Church not to allow
him to preach. At that, James Pierrepont constructed at his
own expense a platform on New Haven green, where a vast
assembly heard Whitefield deliver one of his most celebrated
speeches. It was a conversation with Father Abraham in which
Whitefield would bellow to the sky: "Have you any Congrega-
tionalists up there? any Presbyterians? any Baptists?" After a
pause to allow suspense to generate, Whitefield would report
that Father Abraham had told him, "We know none of these
names up here." This was a pioneering ecumenical pronounce-
ment, but it did not please denominationalists of the day. The
speech caused a split in First Church and James Pierrepont contributed enthusiastically to a new Blue Meeting House (a name
referring to its color) which was built in 1748 by the people
who were adherents of Whitefield. James paid for the episode
by diminished popularity in town, though he kept on as a
selectman until 1773. These events also were the reason for
a split in New Haven church life that lasted for centuries.

Back in Northampton as the children grew, the girls became
conspicuously prettier and the numbers of young preachers troop-
ing to visit the famous theologian increased, and the old

nuisance about money also grew. Sarah almost every night had an extra plate or two to fill at her long dinner table, and small feet had a way of outgrowing shoes. There has turned up in a Scottish bookstore, where it had been slipped into an early Edwards memoir, a receipt in Edwards' own handwriting that indicates how pressed the family was for money as far back as 1742. In those days the town constables were supposed to pay the preacher's wages out of taxes. Sometimes a constable was lax about collecting taxes, and the minister had to wait to be paid. The receipt shows that Edwards had once bypassed the constable and simply taken from a lenient neighbor the portion of his taxes that would have been marked for Edwards' salary. The note says:

> "To Preserved Bartlet Constable this note Returned by you to me, shall be accepted as one pound Six shillings of my salary received of Sam Phelps & me."

It was dated Northampton, May 31, 1742.

In 1744 the family was still pinched, and it was Sarah's turn to try to extract their delayed salary from a constable. Preserved in Northampton still is a hasty scrawl with spelling so bad that it indicates her haste and agitation: "Sir: Mr. Sheldon jest now informs me that you cannot Send all the money at the time. Mr. Edwards is Rid out and therefore I write to Desire you to Send Some as much as you Possibbly can."

They had another pressure on them in this period. Fellow clerics began openly to show their antagonism to Edwards. When he was taking his young daughter Sarah with him to Boston in 1743 they met at the switching station in Brookfield, Massachusetts, Edwards' old opponent, President Thomas Clap of Yale. Cooped up together in a coach all the way to Boston, the men "earnestly disputed." Afterward, Clap reported that Edwards and Whitefield had a scheme to oust some New England clergy and replace them with men from Scotland. Edwards insisted that Clap had picked up "some strange and wonderful Misapprehension" and demanded that Clap publish a retraction. President Clap tartly retorted, "I hope for the future your Time will be better employ'd."

Edwards' running controversy with Charles Chauncy of First Church in Boston was one he rather enjoyed, because he respected Chauncy's intelligence. Chauncy was revolted by the Awakening and said so in a massive, dignified book that Edwards had to admire even though he disagreed with it. When Chauncy prodded the faculty of Harvard to issue a statement deploring Whitefield's methods, Edwards wrote him of his regret that the issue divided "us into two armies, separated and drawn up in battle array, ready to fight with one another, which greatly hinders the work of God."

By now Sarah had learned the costliness as well as the magnificence of being married to an unusual man. Because her husband was totally committed to what appeared to him to be the will of God, he was not cramped by the tiny fears that make another kind of man cautious. Such a man is likely to collide with others who hold differing views of the truth. Fortunately, Sarah had now worked past her earlier need to be approved by everyone. The consistent serenity she had achieved after her crisis made it possible for her to go on lovingly supporting Edwards and giving her children confidence that they were safe at home however chilly the community was toward them.

One afternoon Edwards and Sarah were riding horseback together, enjoying the chance to be alone with each other away from family noises. They had a favorite sandy road that skirted a low bluff on the riverbank. There they stopped and as they watched sheep munching the grass on cleared patches of pasture across the river, Edwards confided to Sarah his growing conviction that no one should join the church unless he made a "profession of godliness." This was an explosive subject.

The Halfway Covenant was a compromise worked out by the Synod of New England from 1657 to 1662. This device allowed the "unawakened" to enjoy part membership so their children could take part in congregational and, even more important, political activities. In colonial society only church members had a vote in the town meetings that were held in April and September to choose the selectmen and tithing men, the sealers of leather, the overseers of weights and measures, the tax collectors, the men who put the town brand on all horses in case they strayed. Town meeting also chose the highway supervisors, who saw that each man put in two days a year helping work on the roads. In small communities where people had been closely bound together for common safety, they cared greatly about having power to influence such decisions. A man took his vote seriously, and when his church membership was questioned, it was a major threat to him.

In the turn of the century Solomon Stoddard had diluted this compromise even more by proposing that the "unregenerate" could take Communion, provided their reputations were not "scandalous." Stoddard wanted to make room for those who weren't ready to claim that they'd had an experience of "regenerating grace." Increase Mather, Harvard's president, had been horrified. The debate between Stoddard and Mather had made "a great noise in the country." Many people would reminisce about that controversy if Edwards were to go ahead in his proposal to restore the sanctity of the Lord's Supper, a transaction that he regarded with utmost awe.

Sarah reported that Edwards "told me that He would not dare ever to admit another person without a profession of real saving religion . . . and spake much of the great difficulties that he expected would come upon Him by reason of his opinion." Edwards then drew up four simple statements a person might make in order to share in the Lord's Supper. All the statements were innocuous. This is one sample: "I hope, I do truly find a heart to give up myself wholly to God, according to the tenor of that covenant of grace which was sealed in my baptism, and to walk in a way of that obedience to all the commandments of God, as long as I live." The other three statements were equally temperate. But Sarah knew that the people would gag at saying even those mild words.

Sarah was most apprehensive about the reaction of their

cousin, friend, and protector, Col. John Stoddard. "Sometimes
we talked of the probability of Colonel Stoddard's disliking my
opposing the opinion and Practice of his Father." It is interesting
that she said *my*, not *his*. Perhaps it was a slip of her pen. Or it
may be that Sarah knew that Stoddard had a particular esteem
for her, even more than for Edwards.

Though she quaked, Sarah realized that she had chosen to
marry the sort of man who did not give in when he believed a
matter of deep principle was at stake.

> I asked him what course he intended to take. He said
> he knew not what. I asked Him if he would not publish
> something expressly handling the subject and vindicating
> his opinion.
> He replied not unless he was forced to it for He did not
> at all love openly to oppose his grandfather in that manner.
> He said to preach against him would be looked upon as a
> great degree of arrogance . . . and much more to print
> against Him. He chose for the present to content Himself
> with giving some occasional Intimations of his opinion that
> People may be thinking of it.

They rode back to town together and like an armada stocking up with water and dried meat for a long campaign, they
began to store up strength. They knew what might happen
when people realized what Edwards thought. As Sarah said: "He
often signified that when he should begin to have occasion to
act on His principles . . . then the Tumult would begin."

There is an amusing aspect to what happened next. They
waited tensely for a hullabaloo when Edwards' book on *Religious Affections* came out. Nothing happened at all. Sarah
reports that "he said to me that he wondered that he had heard
nothing of the people's taking notice that he differed from Mr.
Stoddard." The truth was that the people had not read the
book. Edwards, who was nourished by literature, overestimated
the impact of print on other people. There was no commotion
because his parishioners either didn't read the book, or if they
tried to look at it, didn't understand it. Edwards had made an

error many intellectuals make. They project onto others a capacity for reflectiveness that many people do not have. A situation that would leave a finely turned personality thrumming may leave a less imaginative person merely indifferent. George Whitefield once commented on this when he told of seeing some criminals riding in a cart on their way to the gallows. They were "tossing up who should sit on the right hand of the cart" with no more concern than children who are on their way to buy ice cream.

Sarah continued her narrative: "I had [no] imagination that he desired it should be kept secret and therefore both I and my children often freely spoke of it when we had occasion." She went on to tell how a friend had come up to visit them from New Jersey, bringing reports of the founding of a new college there. When Mr. Edwards told the visitors about the dilemma he faced, he predicted it "was likely [to be] a means of throwing him out of Business and bringing him and his Family to poverty." The guests advised, "You had better run away from these difficulties and accept the place of the President of New Jersey College." But, Sarah concluded, "Mr. Edwards replied He must not run away."

# X

## Time Out
## for Two More Romances

The most agreeable Family I was ever acquainted with.
—*Joseph Emerson*

I am in one continued, perpetual and uninterrupted
hurry.                                    —*David Brainerd*

Before the Edwards drama crested, their children provided
two subsidiary plots. One was humorous, though it did not
seem so to the young man involved. The Reverend Joseph
Emerson of Pepperell, Massachusetts, was dented by the charms
of Esther Edwards and has left an ingratiating diary about his
tribulations. Of all the girls, Esther was most like her mother,
and stamped with Sarah's social skills. She was a luminous
beauty, but more. Her conversation was more entertaining than
the bland chatter of most girls of the era. She was adroit at
drawing out the shy and parrying wits with the intellectual, and
she had an ebullient sense of humor. She dazzled young Mr.
Emerson, and his story gives a revealing glimpse into the
Edwards family scene.

Emerson came of a respected family on the Eastern Coast.
His father, a man of "substantial resources as well as one of
superior scholarship," had come to Ipswich, Massachusetts, in
1636 and married into a family named Waldo. (An eventual
product of this alliance was to be Ralph Waldo Emerson.)
Joseph Emerson, born in 1724, went to Yale and he was returning from the Yale commencement in 1747 when, on the

well-traveled road near Wethersfield, Connecticut, he and his friend Edwards Eels encountered Jonathan Edwards, also cantering back from the festivities in New Haven.

Emerson's mother was related to the Samuel Moody who had figured in the amusing incident the time Edwards was late for the speaking engagement at Portsmouth, New Hampshire, so Edwards was delighted to meet the young man. Confident that Sarah could improvise for unexpected guests, Edwards expansively invited both young men to detour over to Northampton for a visit before they started east to their homes.

After his introduction to Northampton, Emerson wrote in his diary: "Spend the day very pleasant. The most agreeable Family I was ever acquainted with. much of the Presence of God here." The household had to tuck in another unexpected guest while Emerson was there—a Mr. Spencer, who was ordained in Boston to be a missionary to the Indians at Albany. When the young men were ready to return home, Edwards escorted Emerson and his friend Eels across the river, leaving Emerson convinced that "he is certainly a great man."

Back home in Pepperell, our hero could not settle down to work. "Studied some in the morning I had determined to spend the rest of the day in Fasting and Prayer but was interrupted." The reason for the prayer and fasting emerges as Emerson confides: "Mon. 7 Set out some time before day on a journey to Northampton to visit Mrs.* Esther Edwards to treat of marriage."

Though Esther was only in her mid teens, girls married young then, and her charms seem to have been in full bloom. Emerson writes:

> Wednesday 9 I got safe to Northampton, obtained Liberty of the House. Thurs. 10 I spent chief of the day with Mrs. Esther in whose company the more I am the greater value I have for her.

Esther may have been embarrassed by her smitten house guest, for she managed to have an errand the next day, while Emerson

---

* In that time, women of high social rank were all addressed as "Mrs."

occupied himself by copying off some things Edwards had
"lately received from Scotland." He cornered Esther for the
evening, however, and the next day, Saturday, he "spent part of
the Day upon the Business I came about." Sunday "a Mr.
Eaton of Leicester" also turned up and Sarah kept Esther busy
helping entertain the guests. Then church on Sunday inter-
vened. Finally, Emerson had a chance on Monday to propose,
but he "could not obtain from the young lady the least Encouragement to come again." Trying to talk himself into a
cheery attitude toward his reverse, he added:

> I hope the disappointment will be sanctified to me and
> that the Lord will by his Providence order it so this shall
> be my companion for Life.

Dolefully, he rode off home.

> I was considerable melancholly . . . concluded notwith-
> standing . . . to make another trial in the Spring.

The church in Pepperell did not get its money's worth out
of its young minister in the weeks after that.

> Sat. 19 so discomposed I could not study, I could not
> have thought what I have lately met with would have had
> this effect. Fri. 23 I was this Day so pressed down . . . I
> could not fix my mind to do anything at all. . . . Sat. 24
> It seems to be growing upon me. I read a little but chief
> of the day sat meditating on my Troubles.

Interspersed among these entries are notations about sick calls,
committee meetings, the funeral of a child, preaching in a
private house, visiting widows. Emerson plugged along at the
rigamarole of keeping a parish going, but a note of loneliness
is streaked through all his journal.

Esther seems to have been so flabbergasted by this persistent
swain that she turned to her mother to extricate her. Mr. Emerson received a letter

> from Mrs. Sarah Edwards of Northampton who entirely
> discouraged me from taking a journey there again. . . . I
> am disappointed. The Lord teach me [to] be resigned.

He took a while to recover. He had a wedding, went doggedly to committee meetings, tried to take his mind off his disappointment. He wrote: "Tues. 21 Very much out of order. I have a constant faintness at my stomach." By Sunday the second he confesses, in a line that would make any other minister know he had been through a trauma: "I was obliged to preach old sermons all day."

The following Sunday he was still in pain. "Preached on There is no peace saith my God to the wicked. My weakness still continues."

And there Mr. Emerson, with queasy stomach and dashed hopes, departs from our narrative. Two hundred years later, we can feel for him in his rejection. However, he went on to marry an Abigail Hay and have a son who influenced the founding of Mount Holyoke College. The younger Joseph Emerson taught for twenty-one years in a "normal school" in Newburyport—a place where young women were prepared for teaching careers. One of his students was a bouncy little bird of a girl named Mary Lyon. The official biography of her, produced by Mount Holyoke, the college she was to found, says, "Mr. Emerson revealed her to herself."

While the church life in coastal Massachusetts was feeling the reverberations of Esther Edwards' magnetism, another daughter's romance was adding a touching footnote to the Edwards chronicle. Jerusha was, according to her father's description, "a very pleasant and useful member of this household and that was generally esteemed the Flower of the Family." Sweet, generous, impulsive Jerusha was overwhelmed by a young visitor Edwards brought into the house on Thursday, May 28, 1746, unaware that he was bringing tragedy into it.

The guest was David Brainerd, a young zealot who is still being debated. He is a figure almost as controversial as Edwards himself. Some consider him an authentic candidate for saintliness. Others spot neurotic extremes in his personality. There is no doubt that his short life profoundly affected the world missionary enterprise. By the time David Brainerd rode up to the gate on King Street on that May evening he was already, at age twenty-eight, almost a character from folklore.

Brainerd had been born in Haddam, Connecticut, of a substantial family whose house, standing back from the river, overlooked a fine view of groves and fields. His father, an official representative of the king in the provincial government, died when Brainerd was nine. His mother died when he was fourteen. These double deaths may have had much to do with the quirks of character Brainerd was to develop. Though they left him well off financially, so that he was able to send other young men to college with his surplus inheritance, the loss of both parents was a psychic shock.

"Exceedingly distressed and melancholy," Brainerd worked on a farm until he was twenty, making his home with the Haddam pastor who gave him the dubious advice "to stay away from youth and cultivate grave, elderly people." Brainerd later acknowledged that this priggish admonition led him "to proceed . . . at length on a self-righteous foundation." He went off to Yale in 1738, but a severe case of measles sent him home to Haddam in 1739. During this period he was in a crisis of health and morale, much like Edwards' own slump in college. This may have been one reason why Edwards felt drawn toward the younger man. Brainerd, reminiscing about this unattractive period in his life, admitted that he had "contested with the almighty . . . finding fault with his ways of dealing with mankind."

The Awakening stirred him to a kind of religion so fervent that it led to his being expelled from Yale. The emotional ardor of the Whitefield-Tennent brand of religion led Brainerd to form a "cell group" for devotions with a number of friends. One night Brainerd remarked of a certain Yale tutor named Whittlesley that the man "has no more grace than this chair." A nosy freshman lurking outside in the hall heard that impudent comment and raced off to report Brainerd. The rector of the college demanded a public apology. Brainerd retorted that he would not retract in public what he had said in a private conversation. He was expelled, and became a topic of hot discussion throughout New England. In 1742, Brainerd sneaked back into New Haven for the commencement of his class. He probably stayed at James Pierrepont's house. Someone, most likely Edwards himself, has tampered with Brainerd's diary, and a name has been erased so one line reads "lodged at _____." The anonymous censor may have known that Pierrepont was already in trouble for his hospitality to Whitefield and did not want it known that the controversial Brainerd had also been his guest.

Brainerd had a talent for flamboyance. He decided to be an evangelist to the Indians in "the hideous, howling wilderness" west of the coastal colonies. At that time the American colonial churches were not alert about missions. One hundred years earlier, in 1646, the admirable minister of Roxbury, Massachusetts, John Eliot, had pressed back into the surrounding forest and learned to preach to the Indians in their own language. This impressed them so much that Eliot was able to organize more than a dozen communities of "praying Indians." The enterprise had languished after Eliot's death. Only a few British philanthropical societies were still supporting missions to the American Indians, and these were in settled towns, not itinerate ministries. Brainerd persuaded a Scottish group called the Honorable Society for Propagating Christian Knowledge to sponsor him and he plunged off the known maps. Soon the lonely young horseman had become a legend among New England and New Jersey churches.

With no precedent to direct him, Brainerd simply started out to hunt some Indians to convert. He headed for Indian camps reported to be at the forks of the Delaware River. But he picked up some advance gossip that those tribes were scrapping with the white settlers who had pushed in there, so Brainerd concluded that this was not the optimal time to talk in that place about the superiority of the white man's religion. Instead, he plunged into the woods between Stockbridge and Albany. Promptly lost, he spent all night in the open air and on Good Friday of 1743 he confessed to his diary: "My heart was sunk . . . I seemed to have no God to go to."

Fortunately, he next came across "an ingenious young Indian"

named John Wauwaupequuaunt, who happened to know English because he had been raised by a white minister in Long-
meadow, Massachusetts. With John as his guide, Brainerd
crunched through the brush to an Indian colony deep in the
forest where he stayed seven weeks. Woods then were track-
less, except for rare moccasin trails. When it rained, a rider
had no raincoat to protect him—the natural oil in a wool cape
was his only water repellent. Brainerd lived on what he could
hunt or fish for, and his loneliness was colossal. One night he
wrote in his journal of meeting with some Indians on an island
in the Susquehanna River. He had encountered those same
Indians the spring before and they had seemed friendly, so
Brainerd thought he was encouraged to come see them again.
When he returned in September, however, the Indians ignored
him. Nearly one hundred braves were dancing around a fire,
burning deer fat to make the flames spurt "to a prodigious
height." They danced and yelled so loud "they might easily
have been heard two miles or more" and paid no attention at
all to their white visitor. Brainerd morosely watched them, and
finally "crept into a little crib made for corn and there slept."
The next day the Indians spent three more hours doing "hideous charms and Incantations," giving their visitor no opportunity
to preach. He admitted it was "the most burdensome and disagreeable Sabbath that ever I saw." One cannot imagine a
situation in which a sensitive young man would feel more of an
outsider.

He wandered on to another encampment, and again reached
them on a Sunday. "There appeared to be no Sabbath; the children were all at play. I was a stranger in the wilderness and
knew not where to go." He encountered one crazed Indian who
considered himself "a restorer of what he supposed to be the
ancient religion of the Indians." This man loomed before
Brainerd wearing a bearskin coat and bearskin stockings. He was
shaking a dry tortoise shell with corn inside it to make it rattle,
and wore a "great wooden face painted half black, half tawny."
Our young reporter admits: "I could not but shrink away from
it Although it was then noonday and I knew who it was."

That Brainerd came out alive from his wanderings in the forests was in itself an achievement. Medicine men were still powerful then—Brainerd observed many places where "the ground was beat hard as a rock from dancing." These influential Indians did not welcome an outsider who threatened their power over their superstitious constituents.

Also, the physical hardships of travel were great. Brainerd once rode to Stockbridge in December to attend an installation and wrote that he was "very much fatigued with my journey, wherein I underwent great hardship; was much exposed and very wet by falling into a river." After another day of clambering over frozen trails he admits, "Spent the evening in perplexity, a kind of guilty indolence." By November, 1745, he had ridden "more than 3,000 miles since March last" and had baptized twenty-three Indian adults, twenty-four children.

Word about Brainerd's adventures sped about the colonies, and he was invited to speak about them. He even went as far as East Hampton, on Long Island, which was in Edwards' words "the fairest, pleasantest town on the whole Island, and one of its largest and most wealthy parishes." Captivated by Brainerd, the congregation asked him to stay on as its minister. Though the town was very attractive and he would have been in the midst of many old friends, Brainerd "resolved to go on still with the Indian affair." The congregation then called the same Mr. Buell who had lived with the Edwardses, and he stayed there for fifty-two years.

Brainerd was less lonely after this because his Scottish sponsors budgeted enough money for him to take along two other Indians in addition to his clever interpreter. He thought this was a good time for one more try at the Delaware Valley, "a desolate and hideous country above New Jersey; where were very few settlements." This proved a formidable target. It was "the most difficult and dangerous traveling any of us had ever seen. We had scarce anything else but lofty mountains, deep valleys and hideous rocks to make our way through."

In this unpromising place, Brainerd's horse broke its leg and had to be shot. Slogging on by foot, Brainerd reflected, "I can't

get her place supplied for fifty pounds." Though even then a
young man named Nehemiah Greenman, of Southbury, Connecticut, was attending college on a scholarship donated by
Brainerd, this mishap made him feel pinched for money for
the first time in his life, and he sold a teakettle and an iron
pot. An early frost added to their discomfort and the party
spent several bone-chilling nights before they came upon the
shelter of an Indian camp on the riverside.

It was the hunting season, when braves had to go out for the
deer they would urgently need to store for winter, but Brainerd
was so magnetic that the braves stayed home to hear a sermon,
missing a day of hunting. The missionaries pushed on up the
river, though a northeast storm kept them from making fires,
their horses ate some poisonous food, and Brainerd himself
picked up a digestive ailment. Though the region was forbidding,
the Delaware Indians turned out to be even-tempered, with a
stable communal life in longhouses. But Brainerd observed
that "they seemed not to know what they thought of themselves." As converts they were problematical. One named Moses
Tattamy exploited his conversion enough that one of his sons
achieved a Princeton education. He may have been a forerunner
of the "rice Christians" who mixed faith with expediency.

On May 30 after riding 340 miles under harsh conditions,
Brainerd

> rode to Princeton in a very weak state, had such a violent
> fever by the way that I was forced to alight at a friend's
> house and lie down for some time. Near night was visited
> by Mr. Treat, Mr. Beaty and his wife and another friend.
> My spirits were refreshed to see them; but I was surprised,
> and even ashamed that they had taken such pains as to
> ride 30 or 40 miles to see me.

("Beaty" was probably the vigorous minister from Neshaminy,
Pennsylvania, who started life as a peddler and later was on a
committee that was instrumental in founding the first American
life insurance company, which still is thriving.)

This entry suggests a puzzle about Brainerd. Though his

diaries sound glum, his public personality was open and attractive. Edwards had a theory that Brainerd's melancholy came from remorse about the way he had acted at Yale. "He abhorred himself for his imprudent zeal and misconduct at that time." While Brainerd was being charming to many people, a segment of him stood aside. He wrote about one bright Sunday when he had preached on a sunlit hillside to a large, responsive group of people. Another man would have been gratified by so much attention, but David Brainerd later confided to his diary that night: "Was too much crowded with company and conversation and longed to be more alone with God." Edwards, a psychologist before the word was coined, observed of Brainerd that "there were some imperfections which ran through his whole life." Yet, he went on to emphasize, this complex young man was being refined and tested by the process of living. "His grace ripened, the religious exercises of his heart became more and more pure and he more and more distinguishing in his judgement, the longer he lived, he had much to teach and purify him."

In the summer of 1745 when Brainerd preached at the forks of the Delaware, he had results that would have gratified a man of different ego needs, yet his own version of the day was: "I never saw the work of God appear so independent of means as at this time. . . . I could scarce believe He used me as an instrument." The dark night of his soul was shading into a kind of dawn, and he worked harder than ever. To his brother John he wrote in December, "I am in one continued, perpetual and uninterrupted hurry." He also pushed himself strenuously to take his share of responsibility for church government, making tremendous rides just to participate in an ordination or to vote in a meeting. His brother Nehemiah had died of tuberculosis in 1742 and now Brainerd's own body began to pay for the many weeks of exposure and lack of sleep in damp forests. Too late, he realized, as Edwards put it, "that he ought to have taken more thorough care." Brainerd spent a miserable winter as the classic symptoms of tuberculosis slashed away at his body.

Though his voice grew hoarse and swallowing was difficult, he would force himself to preach to his Indians, even as he shook with fever. Fortunately, by now he had come to Cranbury, New Jersey, where kindly Indians welcomed him and helped him build his fourth residence in an Indian colony.

A characteristic of tuberculosis is the alternation of periods of physical prostration with times of remission when the creative energies frantically accelerate. By spring Brainerd dared to think he was better. He wrote on April 21: "I set out on my journey to New England in order (if it might be the will of God) to recover my health by riding." On May 28, 1746, Brainerd turned up in Northampton, and the family welcomed him with no idea that they were receiving disaster into their house. It was not proved until 1868 that tuberculosis was contagious. Before that time everyone thought it was a hereditary disease because it pounced upon whole families. Brainerd had perked up enough to believe that he was going to be well. Edwards wrote that he was "vastly better than, by his own account, he had been in the winter."

The sunniest side of Brainerd's nature was forward when he came to the Edwards house, and he promptly captivated the whole family. Edwards wrote that they

> found him remarkably sociable, pleasant and entertaining
> in his conversation. . . . We enjoyed not only the benefit
> of his conversation but had the comfort and advantage of
> hearing him pray in the family from time to time.

Particularly impressed was Jerusha, the daughter Edwards had described to Erskine as "a very pleasant and useful member of this household . . . the Flower of the Family." Brainerd was then twenty-eight years old and Jerusha was only seventeen, but the whole family could see that, as Edwards put it, she was "a person of much the same spirit" as Brainerd.

The young man singled out Jerusha, telling her that his favorite sister had the same name. (Jerusha Brainerd Spencer had named her son David Brainerd after her brother.) As Jerusha helped her mother carry in the vegetable tureens and bought more hot water for the teapot, she intently watched the guest.

When the family bowed their heads at the table, Edwards invited Brainerd to say the blessing. Edwards later wrote:

> I know not that ever I heard him so much as ask a blessing or return thanks at table but there was something remarkable to be observed.

Though Sarah Edwards shared the general appreciation for their winning guest, she noticed how thin he was, and how bright his eyes were. The next day she suggested to Dr. Mather that he stop in to see Brainerd. The stethoscope had not yet been invented, but the case history of tuberculosis could be read by a seasoned observer. Dr. Mather, an experienced doctor by this time, examined Brained, then came straight to the point and said "he could give him no encouragement." After he had absorbed that verdict, Brainerd decided to make a last trip to Boston to wind up his affairs and arrange for his mission to pass along to others. Then Jerusha did a thing that must have been unusual for those times, and her mother, surprisingly, responded. Jerusha asked to go along with Brainerd, and her mother let her do it.

The couple started on June 9, traveling slowly. Along the road they met a group of clergy and joined them for the rest of the way to Boston. The beauty of the weather and the company of Jerusha made Brainerd realize that he "desired the continuance of life." Through roses and flowering shrubs and all the blandishments of early summer, they moved east and came to Boston on June 12. Brainerd told his journal: "God appeared excellent, His ways full of pleasure and peace."

Elated by the joy of these days, Brainerd felt his health had surged back and he bustled about Boston introducing Jerusha to his friends and meeting hers. But by June 18 he was jolted again. Doctors concluded that "the ulcers in his lungs had broken." Jerusha wrote to the family: "On Thursday he was ill with a violent fever. . . . [We were] up with him until one or two o'clock, expecting every hour would be his last." Brainerd's brother Israel was notified of his illness and he hastened up to Boston from Connecticut. He brought news that rocked Brainerd, for he reported that Jerusha Spencer had suddenly died down in Haddam. This was a fearful blow to the brother who had "a peculiarly dear affection for her." Boston extended itself to cheer up the grieving Brainerd. Gifts poured in. He was given three dozen Bibles to take back to his Indians, as well as cash and pledges that made secure the future of his mission. Then the cruel caprice of his disease gave Brainerd another false reprieve.

On July 19 he felt well enough to put in a day of church going that would seem strenuous even to a healthy man. He rode in a chaise in the morning to hear Joseph Sewall preach. Then he took Communion, and the afternoon saw him going out again to hear Thomas Prince conduct the second service. When it was time for David and Jerusha to start the trip back to Northampton, a troop of admirers went along to the edge of town to say good-by. Taking advantage of the cool of the afternoon's low-slanting sun, they started late in the day. To Jerusha's relief, Israel went along to help her. She needed his assistance, for Brainerd was "extremely tired and faint on the road."

After traveling only a cautious sixteen miles most days, they finally made it back to Northampton. There Brainerd had "a continual desire to improve time." He wrote many letters, corrected his journal, contributed the preface for a book about to be published in Boston. Jerusha riding beside him, he even continued to take exercise, going out on horseback. On September 2 the strong vein of sociability in his nature made Brainerd go out to the Public Lecture, for he wanted to see all the old friends who had turned up in town for that event. But, as Edwards reported, "it was the last time he ever went out at our gate." Two days later Brainerd had to give up climbing stairs, and Sarah had to fix up a bedroom downstairs for him.

She was pregnant again and the next weeks were grim for her. Illness in any house is taxing for the mother, and it was harder in those days when bandages had to be tediously made, then laundered for reuse. Washing and all forms of nursing were more awkward than they are now. Sarah was additionally anguished to see Jerusha under such strain, for Jerusha lashed herself to do all the nursing, though others offered to help.

The household chores increased because Brainerd's brothers Israel and John came to see him, and two other young men chose that awkward time to arrive to talk with Edwards about their interest in preparing for the ministry. That Sarah survived those weeks speaks of how much she must have drawn upon her deep devotional resources.

The day of the visit of the young ministerial aspirants, September 29, was actually a pleasant one. Brainerd quizzed the young men about their sense of calling to the vocation and all the family gathered with them around the bed while they sang together Psalm 102.

One would like to know how Sarah handled her smaller children on the day the pale invalid on the first floor called the children in one by one and whispered to each in turn: "When you see my grave, then remember what I said to you while I was alive; then think with yourself how that man who lies in that grave . . . warned me to prepare for death." Did the children have nightmares after they went to bed that night? Or had the sermons they had heard every Sunday of their memory, spoken in the dear, familiar voice of their father, prepared them to be matter-of-fact about the fragility of life, the nearness of the grave?

Fortunately, the family was spared the trial of having to cope with a delirious patient: "Until the day before his death he had the free use of his reason . . . excepting that at times he appeared a little lost for a moment." For Jerusha, the most strenuous scene came on the morning of October 4. While she was puttering with his pillow or perhaps coaxing him to have a cup of tea, Brainerd said: "Dear Jerusha, are you willing to part with me? I am quite willing to part with you, though if I had thought I should not see you and be happy with you in another world, I could not bear to part with you."

On October 8 a friend came to call, and Brainerd talked with him, then continued late at night in earnest talk with his

brother John. Brainerd asked John to suggest to the Indians
in his congregation that they join with the Scottish preachers
in Edwards' plan for a united day of prayer. (Later the Indians
did so, "with great cheerfulness and unanimity.") The next day
Brainerd died, saying, "It is another thing to die than people
imagine."

Edwards with inadvertent snobbery reported that in the tranquil cemetery which slopes toward a wide view of hills "eight
neighboring ministers and seventeen other gentlemen of liberal
education and a great concourse of people attended" the services.
Using as his text, "True saints, when absent from the body are
present with the Lord," Edwards eulogized the young man who
had made a tragic impression on his own family.

Jerusha, who had nursed Brainerd for nineteen weeks, then
caved in herself and the whole grim matter had to be endured
again. Her resistance was greater, and she was acutely ill only
five days. But on February 14, Valentine's Day, Jerusha died.
It happened at 5 A.M. on a Sunday and on that day, for the
first time in his life, Edwards preached an old sermon out of
his "barrel" to his own congregation. He used one he had given
seven years before, on The Book of Job. So for the first time
there was a small stone bearing the Edwards name in that peaceful knoll in the cemetery at Northampton.

David Brainerd had intended his papers to be destroyed, but
his friends in Boston persuaded him to turn all his materials
over to Edwards. At that point Edwards could not have forced
himself to do any other writing but he comforted himself by
rummaging through Brainerd's papers and shaping them into
a memoir. Published in 1747, this modest project surprisingly
became Edwards' most widely read book and it had long reverberations. In England it was discovered by William Carey,
a brilliant, self-educated shoemaker. Inspired by that story,
Carey had the idea of founding the London Missionary Society.
Then in 1806 a group of Williams College students were walking in a field near their campus when a rain came up. They
dived into a haystack for shelter and there, while they waited
for the squall to stop, they talked. One of the group, Samuel

Mills, had just been reading about Brainerd and Carey, and he told the rest about them. Moved by the stories, they decided to become America's first foreign missionaries. All of them went on to Andover Seminary and in June, 1810, took their plan to the General Association of Congregational Ministers. To deal with this unprecedented suggestion, the ministers set up the American Board of Commissioners for Foreign Missions. A major figure on that first board was a son of Mary Edwards, Jerusha's sister, so the Brainerd influence came full circle, back to the house in Northampton again.

In spite of all the upheaval Brainerd had caused in the Edwards house, all the emotional toll, and the crowning anguish of losing Jerusha, Edwards could say:

> I would not conclude my observations . . . without acknowledging with thankfulness the gracious dispensation of providence to me and my family, in so ordering it that he should be brought to my house in his last sickness.

How much this ordeal cost Sarah is told in the fact that the baby she had been carrying proved to be her only puny one. On May 6, two months after Jerusha died, Elizabeth was born. She had rickets and was always frail, but the family doted on her. She appeared when they all needed a new channel for their deepest feelings.

Sarah experienced then for the first time the grief that often struck down other mothers. The ache for a lost child is a form of bereavement like no other. This loss was peculiarly poignant because it happened on Valentine's Day, one of the merriest days in the colonial calendar, when there was much ado about parties and secret slipping of elaborate handmade cards under doorsteps. (In 1746 all of social New York reverberated when Mrs. James Alexander, a grande dame, refused to let her daughter accept a valentine from the new young organist of Trinity Church.) Holidays are hard to bear after a loss, for they emphasize the changes the year has made since the same date twelve months before, and it is lonely to be sad on a festive occasion. For Sarah, Valentine's Day now became an annual reminder of a scar she would carry forever.

# XI

## Present: Tense

At last we arrive at an entire annihilation of ourselves,
and an absolute acquiescence and complacence in the will
of God, which afford the only full answer to all our doubts,
and the only radical cure for all our evils and perplexities.
—*David Hartley* (*1705–1757*)

What component gives a town, a church, a corporation, a
college, its distinction, so that one is yeasty and hopeful, another drab and cantankerous? What causes the youngsters of
one city all to wish to return there to live, while another town
has no partisans? There may have been an atmospheric factor
that made Northampton from its earliest days a community
given to quarrels. Perhaps some combination of genes among
the founding families led to clashes. Once relationships curdle,
all exchanges that flow from them are affected. The bitter word
once shouted, the dish smashed in anger, the cheek reddened
with a slap, the love withdrawn, the climactic scene played—
the emotional mark of such scenes lingers.

Superficially, it can be explained that Northampton had been
divided between a "court party," which had wealth, land, and
authority, and the country people, who resented the power the
first group had over town and church. The two sides habitually
collided on issues and kept a suspicious eye on each other between controversies. Other towns with similar social alignments
did not have such frictions as Northampton appears to have
had. In 1677 when the church got a new bell, the village em-

powered Enos Kingsley to sue for "the wheat sent down by Mr. Stevens" (to pay for the new church bell), "which he pretends was spoiled and so gives no account for it." In 1656, Joseph Parsons sued James Bridgman for slander because he had called Mrs. Parsons a witch. (She turned out to be, actually, a sleepwalker.) In 1658, a year notable because that was when the town built a boat to use on river crossings, there was "a breach or rent in town concerning the Lord's days meetings." Later, there was a prolonged quarrel over the office of measurer of land. Two men were asked to take it, but each refused to serve. There was prolonged bickering in the area about the border between Massachusetts and Connecticut. Edwards was to point out:

> The contentions which have been among you, since I first became your pastor, have been one of the greatest burdens I have laboured under . . . not only the contentions you have had with me, but those you have had with one another, about your land and other concerns.

Edwards' problem was compounded by a rising wave of resentment at the clergy that was a general condition throughout the colonies. As early as 1643, Henrie Walton, of Lynn, Massachusetts, was taken to court for saying that "he had as Leeve to hear a Dogg Barke as to heare Mr. Cobbett Preach." Such cockiness on the part of many individuals foreshadowed the Revolutionary spirit. Rich and successful now, the colonies did not need to be told what to do by Hookers and Mathers. One church record of June, 1725, reported:

> Some evil-minded persons placed a Sturgeon of about 8 feet in length on the Pulpit floor where it lay undiscovered until the Lord's Day following . . . which occasion'd them to perform their Exercise in the Orchard.

In Sarah's home church of New Haven in 1738, Timothy Hutchinson was "required to make humble confession of sin for smiling in church." And the Episcopal scare, stirred up by Timothy Cutler's departure from Yale, made the founders of First Church in Waterbury, Connecticut, so jittery that before they would hire Mark Leavenworth as their minister they made him post a bond of £500 on the promise that he wouldn't turn Episcopalian. (Their ground for suspicion was that Leavenworth's wife had a cousin who was Episcopalian.)

An Albany preacher who offended his people found on his doorstep one Monday morning "a club, a pair of old shoes, a crust of black bread and a dollar." The minister read this as a hint to leave town, so he did. Lemuel Briant was dismissed from John Adams' church in Braintree, Massachusetts, on the charge that he was "light and gay." And a minister in Pomfret, Connecticut, was suspended by the Ministers' Association because he had preached a sermon "which we have very good grounds to believe was not of his own composition." (This charge might remove some clergy from their pulpits today.)

In the earlier years when small groups of settlers had to stand together in order to survive the rigors of the wilderness they had to define strictly the terms for their collective life. They were in an unusual way bound up in one another's welfare, so they had to draw up firm rules. Bachelors were fined for keeping house alone. A person was fined three shillings if he stood outside the meetinghouse, chatting, while services were going on. Parents were required to teach their children the town laws. It all made for group solidarity when solidarity could mean the difference between survival or death. But times had eased.

The earlier austerities of the church were beginning to be resented. The first settlers found virtue in being as bored and uncomfortable as the human frame could endure during worship. Meetinghouses were so cold that Communion bread would freeze, and a pastor had to keep baptismal water in a flask beneath his coat so it would be warm enough to use on a baby's head. People sat through paralyzing sermons several hours long, and after the sermon came town announcements, baptism, the offering, and a song lined out from the *Bay Psalm Book*. After the benediction no one was allowed to wiggle until the clergyman stiffly strode down the aisle. However, congregations were sensibly asking whether it was necessary to be flagellated in church in this way. In Hadley, near Northampton, they had even dared put a stove in the meetinghouse. A Quaker was tarred and feathered for pointing out that church people worshiped the Sabbath, not God, but the issue he raised did not go away.

Another squabble in churches concerned music. The first settlers, intent on kicking off all traces of the liturgy of the church they had left behind, had abolished all music except psalms. In 1723 a book was printed which gave both notes and words for psalms. People complained, "If we begin to sing by rule, the next thing will be to pray by rule." In England, Handel was turning out his mighty works for organ, and enough people wanted to see organs introduced in America that a Harvard senior thesis in 1730 asked, "Do organs excite a devotional spirit?" Edwards himself liked music, and encouraged his people to sing, but even that matter was an abrasive one.

The people in Northampton also chafed at Edwards' many errands out of town. For that day of difficult transportation, he did travel a remarkable amount. He had even gone down to East Hampton, on Long Island, to preach an installation sermon for young Buell, when that was the last jumping-off place. It was an attractive village, prospering in whale trade, but a visitor who came there by horseback had to wait as long as two days for the ferry at Lyme, Connecticut, to take him to Orient Point, and once on the island, he had a considerable ride farther. But the people who grumbled about Edwards' many absences did not realize that it was essential for him to get away to be spiritually replenished for such a taxing parish.

One amusing form of the rising anticlericalism centered on the subject of wigs. These were heavy, hot, and expensive creations, probably invented by a bald man, and they cost at least £10 a year to maintain in good condition, so they had become a sign of rank. The church in West Newbury, Massachusetts, in 1752 met solemnly to "deal with our brother Richard Bartlett . . . our said brother refuses communion with the church for no other reason but because the pastor wears a

wigg." Edwards owned two wigs, which in his methodical way
he catalogued as "One best. Ditto inferior." This was one more
matter in which he did not endear himself to the man who
worked hard with his hands and wore coarse hand-woven shirts
over deerskin breeches.

Sarah was not easy to understand during all this. She knew
that eyes were peering at the parsonage to note every sign of
extravagance, yet she did a curious thing, almost defiantly, as
if she enjoyed the gasps it caused. Edwards spent £11 for a
gold chain and locket for a gift for her. He may have earned
some money for writing up the experience she had recited to
him in 1742 and felt she deserved a dividend from that. Or the
two of them may have reached a secret level of joy together
which he wanted to mark with a brilliant symbol—it would
have been like him to make such a tender gesture, so absorbed
in the primary relationship that he never gave thought to the
reaction of the townspeople. But Sarah, alert to social nuances,
wore the showy gift. Why?

In 1747 the nerves of Northampton were rasped because of
King George's War, the American phase of the conflict which
had begun in 1731 because of a bizarre incident in which an
English master mariner's ear was cut off when his ship was
boarded by some Spanish. It was known as the Jenkins' ear
incident and ultimately developed into the War of the Austrian
Succession, involving not only England, France, Spain, and
other European nations but making reverberations in the
American colonies. The Indians, who were allies of the French,
pestered the English colonial settlements. It happened that
one hot August day in nearby Southampton, Massachusetts,
Elisha Clark was threshing grain in his barn when Indians
killed and scalped him. In May, 1748, they swooped down there
again and tomahawked Noah Pixley as he was leading his cows
out to pasture. Even young Jonathan Judd, in the nearby parish,
fled to the safety of Suffield, Connecticut.

In June, Colonel Stoddard had a stroke while he was in
Boston attending the General Court and he asked that Sarah
come to take care of him. This is interesting. There were many

women in Boston who would have leaped at a chance to help
so rich a man. (Stoddard had thirty-five shirts, a gold watch
worth £150, and an enormous estate.) Did Stoddard want
Sarah with him then because in her person she conveyed
assurance of the reality of God? Stoddard, a faithful worshiper
all his life, may have needed at that point to be sure his God
really existed. Or did he simply want a nurse of Sarah's gentle
grace? She may have seemed to him, too, an extraordinary
woman.

It always takes organizing when a mother leaves a large
family. Menus must be planned, laundry done, lists of instructions left. The baby, Betty, was a problem because her mother
had been her world to that frail child. However, Mrs. Samuel
Phelps, who had stepped in to help when Sarah had briefly
disintegrated in 1742, offered to take the baby. Elisha Pomeroy
volunteered to ride along as Sarah's escort. So for a change
it was Sarah who cantered off, and Edwards who supervised
back home. They all soon realized that the house was without
its heartbeat.

On June 22, Edwards wrote her, addressing her as "My dear
Companion" and telling first how the baby was doing at Mrs.
Phelps's house. "The first two or three days before she was
well acquainted, she was very unquiet but now more quiet
than she used to be at Home." He added a request that Sarah
bring a cheese along with her from Boston, and concluded,
"We have been without you almost as long as we know how
to be." So, when Stoddard died, she hastened home to the
man who needed her most.

The funeral was the largest seen in the town for years. Edwards preached on "A Strong Rod Broken and Withered"
(Ezek. 19:12) and he characteristically chose that time to say
an unpopular thing. In front of the biggest gathering of busi-
nessmen and land speculators ever collected in his meetinghouse, he lashed out at leaders who are of

> a narrow, private spirit that may be found in little tricks
> and intrigues to promote their private interest, who will
> shamefully defile their hands to gain a few pounds, are

not ashamed to nip and bite others, grind the faces of the poor.

He spoke of how Stoddard had represented the best qualities of leadership, and contrasted him with the men who misused authority. Even though she trembled to hear him, Sarah knew he had to say this sometime and that now, with his protector dead, he had taken the risk.

The moods of New Englanders are delicately hinged to weather. Nowhere else is winter so trying, the mud season so endless, spring so giddy, summer so brief, fall so glorious. Tuned to the caprices of weather, the New Englanders' moods swing as the climate does. The year 1749 was one of the spooky extremes. The winter was unusually severe. Mill River had frozen over by early October. The town was smothered by six feet of snow that lingered monotonously for months. Then in the spring the bridge washed out. (Some jokesters made a stunt of the flood. They rowed across the river to Hadley, passed a rope from their boat through a tavern window, and anchored it on the table in the bar room, to general hilarity.) The gray weeks dragged out, chill rains slanting over stubble fields, maples gauntly swaying in the harsh winds. On April 1, a date low in town morale, Edwards undiplomatically hurled at his people a sermon based on Jer. 23:29: "Is not my word like fire, says the Lord, and like a hammer which breaks the rock in pieces?"

Then the summer was the worst on record. There was drought all over New England. Corn parched in the fields. Ministers pleaded with God to send rain. Finally, in late August, a rain came at last, when nerves were at their last notch. In Boston, Thomas Prince on August 24 gave thanks for "the extraordinary reviving rains, after the most distressing drought which has been known among us in the memory of any living." In Northampton, minister and people were so hostile that they even gave up trying to hold Communion services.

Though the chopping off of a relationship is always poignant, there is a special quality of tragedy in estrangement between pastor and parish. Edwards was clumsy at social calls, unable to ingratiate himself with facile small talk, but when one of his people met a deep experience, he was there, solidly and pastorally. In the dark hours of watch over a feverish child, when people really needed him, Edwards would be on hand. Trying to describe this, he had written:

> When a minister and his people are united in love, no earthly connection, if we except that of marriage and those subsisting between the nearest relations by blood, is so near and intimate.

To a minister with such a view of his bonds with his congregation, feuding with his people was the ultimate sadness.

One factor that sliced between Edwards and his parishioners was their irritation over his loftiness. The majesty of his mind had made the name of Northampton known across the ocean and in every college in the colonies, but it was hard to take in daily contact. The gap between his soaring expectations and the level on which most people live made him a mystery to his neighbors.

He also grated on them with his campaign against taverns. Tension between church and tavern was not new. The first town meeting, which had instructed the town agent "to endeavor to obtain a minister," had also debated "a proper course about preventing an excess of liquors in coming to our town and of cider." In 1700, Medad Pomeroy had been licensed to keep a tavern near the pillory—that was a smart location, for it offered free entertainment when gabbing housewives or other picayune offenders were ignominiously displayed. Edwards did not realize that a tavern provided a club, a gathering place, where a man for the cost of a penny for a quart of beer could hear the news, participate in discussions or games of checkers, help himself to one of the long-stemmed clay pipes that were kept on a public rack. (In the interest of sanitation, the smoker broke off an inch or two of stem before settling down to puff.) In locked-in New England, a public common room was essential for village community. Taverns also offered entertainment to spice the uneventful New England winters. A "learned pig" said to be worth $1,000 was exhibited in one Northampton tavern, astonishing audiences with its ability to distinguish colors, do card tricks, tell time. Dancing school was held there, and once the people did ninety-two jigs, fifty-two contra dances, forty-two minuets, and seventeen hornpipes in a single strenuous evening. When the Clarke Tavern was built on Hawley Street in 1746, it provided a necessary headquarters for the judges and lawyers who came for the General Court sessions. A man of Edwards' tidy mind ought to have appreciated the symmetry in the fact that the public schools were supported by fines for drunkenness. He also used the services of the tavern as a center for mail distribution. But Edwards, whose recreation was to think in solitude, did not understand why most people enjoyed the taverns. Their owners, convivial, popular men, were powerful leaders in the community, and it was not strategic to oppose them in the way Edwards did.

He antagonized another group who were to close in on him gleefully when he was in trouble. Though some clergy found him an inspiration and soul companion, Edwards annoyed the routine minister. Some resented Edwards because they sensed that he was more profound than they were and that he made more of his vocation than they did. The mediocre workman always dislikes a man who works harder. He is threatened in this laziness by a man of driving dedication. Other clergymen were annoyed by the contrast between their trivial busyness, and the emphasis Edwards gave to the same work. If he grated on the lazy minister, Edwards also pricked the pompous ones with such pronouncements as:

Pride is the worst viper that is in the heart . . . the most hidden, secret and deceitful of all lusts.

A minister who slickly manipulated people, with his own popularity as his aim, could not have welcomed Edwards' blast:

The day of doom will be that moment . . . when every person must announce his real motives.

Edwards honestly worried about the way he snowed people by his intelligence. On the inside cover of his *Notes on Natural Science*, he had written as a youth:

> Let it not look as if I was much read . . . never to dispute for things that I cannot handsomely retreat [from], upon conviction of the contrary.

He tried to be less awesome, but it was hard. So a group of enemies coalesced in the ministerial association. One who actively worked against him was Ashley, of the church in Deerfield. (As a result, the church in Deerfield split, and the faction who thought Ashley had been unjust to Edwards founded a church in Greenfield.) By the time the clash between Edwards and his parish had reached a point where it needed arbitration by the Ministers' Association, the clergy themselves were divided about him.

In the town, gossips clacked. Despite the high toll of childbirth, there were many widows in New England villages. They were a self-assured group, grandly protected by laws which gave widows unusual rights. Widows were the only women allowed a vote. They were allowed to carry on their husband's business without the apprenticeship required of most people going into the same trade. And they had lots of time to talk.

Tea-drinking was the great indoor sport of that time. After 1720 when tea was introduced in the colonies, the chief afternoon recreation was traipsing to the neighbors for tea. China was scarce, so each lady would carry her own tiny spoon, saucer, and handleless cup, shaped like the ones used in China, where sea captains had discovered tea. The minister and his family provided topics for conversation over many a teacup. Another arena for the gossip was a quilting party. Women quilted in neighborhood groups, taking turns helping each household to produce one of these lovely pieces of equipment. They would sit facing inward at a square table, doing the easy stitches that required many fingers but little thought. So they were free to chat as they sewed, and at these sessions the Edwardses were thoroughly discussed.

Sarah had been conspicuous because she never gossiped. Hopkins claimed that "when she heard persons speaking ill of others she would say what she thought she could in truth and justice, in their excuse." So the gossips had to scratch for any scraps of indiscreet conversation to hold against her. Nevertheless, she was a target of resentment for one reason out of her control. It is inevitable for women to resent another woman who seems too good to be true. As Max Beerbohm suggests in his 1918 essay, *Quia imperfectum*, most of us resent perfection. We find a man such as Goethe boring because he was unrelievedly efficient and productive. We prefer a character with flaws we recognize as like our own—tardiness or a tendency to mislay keys or to be grumpy at breakfast. Naturally, other women looked for a chance to pounce on Sarah Edwards. She had never lost a baby. She had kept her looks, when most women in that day sagged at thirty. Other husbands chose to go alone to barn-raisings or ordinations, but Edwards openly considered his wife a delight and wanted her to be with him. Their daughters were pretty, popular, and helpful in the house. Sarah Edwards was simply too fortunate, and other people could not help feeling jealous of her.

It is easy to understand why people bristled at Edwards, who was so stiff and secretive, given to inexplicable thrusts such as the gift of the gold locket to Sarah. He bumbled badly in the famous incident of the "bad book," when he discovered that the young people in town were passing around a midwives' manual to chortle over behind the barn. It had been the month of March, 1744, and March is always a dreary time, when things go wrong and judgment falters. Edwards always slumped in March, so this time he had stupidly read aloud in church the names of those who were to appear at the investigation, without distinguishing between witnesses and those supposedly culprits, and this detonated a colossal row. Later, even he realized that he had made a blunder. Among his papers are listed alternatives that he might have taken. On the back of a shopping list for a trip he made soon after to his parents' home in Windsor, Edwards wondered

whether I ought to have done anything about it as the
pastor of the church . . . whether I ought to have gone
and talked privately with them.

Hindsight could not help him. The damage had been done.

Then he asked the town "to pay the cost of bringing Mr.
Edwards his daughter from Brookfield." Naturally they turned
that down. It was a silly request. He gratuitously made people
bristle when he said he disapproved of the way they spent long
winter evenings going from house to house,

spending the hours in unprofitable conversation with no
other object than to amuse themselves. It is wrong to
spend so many long evenings chatting in one another's
chimney corners.

He also pointed out that when he visited in houses he noticed
that his people had few books, commenting that "through
their unwillingness to be at a little expense, they miss reading."
Looking back at these mistakes, he confided to his friend,
Gillespie, in Carnock, Scotland:

One thing contributed to bring things to such a pass at
Northampton was my youth and want of more judgement
. . . my confidence in myself was a great injury to me; but
in other respects my diffidence of myself injured me.

He reminded himself to save his energies for big issues, and
not to tangle with trivial bickering. "God does not call us to
have our spirits ceaselessly engaged in opposition and stirred up
in anger unless it be on some important occasions," he used
to like to say.

Two persons precipitated the final crisis. The first was Seth
Pomeroy, described as "very high in liberty." There are some
kinds of people who are chemically incompatible, who cannot
help clashing. So it was with Edwards and Pomeroy. A duplicate of Pomeroy in a later day was Theodore Roosevelt.
Pomeroy was a war lover, impulsive, hotheaded, a man's man.
He was to roar off to serve in the Revolution when he was
sixty-nine. To Pomeroy, a man like Edwards seemed pale and

prissy, and Edwards' kind of work, long hours cooped up indoors, looked like lazy malingering. Their very glands collided.

Finally, an uncontrollable quirk of circumstances was introduced into the picture: Joseph Hawley.

This young man was from a substantial family in whom a streak of strangeness had shown before. His father, a cultivated squire who read Latin and Greek, had suddenly slashed his own throat on June 1, 1735, putting a cloud over the Awakening. Hawley's mother wouldn't let her son marry until he was thirty, and then resented it so much that she divided the house, retreated into her own side, and ignored her daughter-in-law. Though this genetic endowment was unpromising, the younger Hawley seemed to be a reliable citizen. He practiced law, taught school, and in 1747 he became First Selectman. Yet he was sick, and his delusions centered most bitterly on the minister. Slithering through the town, scattering slander, Hawley was most responsible for the final wave of opinion that overwhelmed Edwards.

The mind of the psychotic often fixes upon a person of prominence. This is the fact that haunts the secret service men charged with the safety of a president. Any celebrity is vulnerable. The towering man represents the qualities of the archetypical father. Any man who is a strong, authoritative figure risks the hatred of someone whom he may not even know. We will hear more of Hawley.

The final explosion came over the question Edwards had told Sarah about on their horseback ride together—the matter of who was qualified to be a church member. Edwards, still hoping to meet the emotional antagonisms with rational reconciliation, asked permission to preach about his reasons for taking his stand on church membership. He asked to speak

> not as an act of authority, or as putting the power of . . .
> the whole counsel of God out of my hand, but for peace's
> sake.

Irritably, the parish rejected this request. Next, he proposed that October 15, 1749, be a day of fasting and prayer that

God would have mercy on this church, under its present dark and sorrowful circumstances; that he would forgive the sins of both minister and people.

The people were too cross to allow even God to intervene.

Edwards then tried to make his case through a book. He lashed a Boston printer to strike off copies promptly, and to avoid a wait for them to be delivered, the Edwardses' great friend and next-door neighbor, Col. Timothy Dwight, went to Boston to get the book. Twenty copies were dispersed around town, and again Edwards, who revered the printed word, over-estimated its impact on other people. He also made a blunder, urging that "none be allowed to cast a ballot who had not read it." This demand made many people furious.

Leadenly, the year 1750 began. Church was a hollow ordeal for pastor and people. Edwards continued to work over his sermons until they were burnished brilliantly. Sarah, watching the stony faces in the pew, knew that few people were listening receptively. She also felt cold eyes surveying her thickened waist, for at this inconvenient time, or perhaps because of it, she was pregnant again. At a time when so much was hostile in the world outside, their relationship within the warm world of their marriage had extra meaning. They needed the comfort of each another as never before. But the pregnancy was a complication in such a strenuous year.

At 8:30 A.M. on April 8, a Sunday, Sarah delivered a son, Pierpont.* It is not surprising that this was the scamp of the Edwards children. He was to have a distinguished career, but there was an unsavory streak in Pierpont. His will disclosed some illegitimate children, and his character showed an un-evenness that may reflect the heavy strain his mother was under as she carried him. For the last time, a trundle bed was slid out from under the parents' bed, and kept near enough so the new mother could be alert during the night for each sniffle,

---

* With the naming of this baby, the confusion about the spelling of the family name is confounded. Many primary sources, including Sarah's will, use this spelling, but other branches of the family continued the "Pierrepont" form.

each whimper of demand from the baby to be fed. Depleted by pregnancy and emotionally lacerated, Sarah reached that point of fatigue where one breaks fingernails frequently and is inclined to weep at a trivial mishap such as a sticky door lock. So she caved in with a psychosomatic response to all the pressure—and had rheumatic fever when the baby was two months old.

The worst hours of the week were on Sunday. The door of the meetinghouse served as town bulletin board, where notices of new laws, sales, marriage banns, and town meetings were posted. As people saw Sarah and her children approach the church, they would fall silent and earnestly study the notices on the church doors. Then the hours of worship would be a mockery.

Edwards refused to carry the controversy into the worship hours, for he believed human bickerings were out of place in that lofty context. He explained: "The state of the people has been obviously such that . . . it would have been the occasion of tumult on that holy day." So he decided to use his Thursday-night lectures as a forum. Working over his case with infinite pains, he went down to deliver it, and found only a handful of people there. The following week, however, word had traveled beyond the town, and the curious had come from miles around to peer at the Northampton scandal. A few were as callous as if they were at a theater; others were neighbors seriously concerned about the issues. Edwards noticed that his second lecture, February 22, "was also attended thinly by my own people but by a great number of strangers."

The controversy shredded the town. Of the prominent Lyman family, four who were entitled to vote were hotly opposed to Edwards, and one stayed loyal to him. Edwards reported to his Scottish friend Erskine:

> There is a number whose hearts are broken at what has come to pass. . . . It is thus with one of the principal men of the parish, viz. Col. Dwight; and another of our principal men, viz. Dr. Mather, adheres very much to me.

It is significant that Dr. Mather, who knew the family on the deepest level, was fearlessly their friend. He had presided at the births of the babies and stood close through the deaths of Jerusha and Brainerd. He knew them as no one else did. His loyalty never swerved. When Mather died in 1779, his tombstone inscription suited his stout spirit:

> Corruption earth and worms
> Shall but refine this flesh
> Til my triumphant spirit comes
> To put it on afresh.

Though the tension told on all the Edwards children, two of the daughters found courageous beaux just when they needed them most. The oldest daughter, Sarah, was courted by Elihu Parsons, a Yale graduate, who came from a substantial family. His grandfather ran a profitable sawmill, his father had been a deacon at the time the new meetinghouse was built, and the family owned fifty-four acres of juicy meadowland and had a handsome house. Though it was an unpromising spring for romance, and many must have hooted at him, Parsons was a strong, steady man of thirty-one, and he was not intimidated. On June 11, 1750, he married young Sarah.

Mary was chosen by the boy next door, the son of Colonel Dwight. Young Timothy Dwight was a genial giant, six feet, four inches tall, weighing 250 pounds, with hazel eyes and a fresh, fair coloring that contrasted to the darkly flashing beauty of Mary. (She was so tiny that her suitor would amuse friends by holding her on the palm of his hand, at arm's length.) Young Dwight had been the first white child born in Vermont, for his father commanded forty men in a fort, made of hewed yellow pine, up in a risky outpost. There the older Dwight had distinguished himself as a soldier when he held the upper reaches of the river with four swivel-mounted guns, one cannon, and some Mohawks who made a hobby of fighting River Indians. The Mohawks were rather trying allies. Dwight once complained to John Stoddard that "the Indians daily call upon me for shirts, pipes, bullets and powder, flints and many other things."

Colonel Dwight returned to practice law in Northampton as well as to become merchant, selectman, and judge of the Court of Common Pleas in addition to overseeing the family's large land holdings. His son had graduated from Yale in 1744 and returned to help in his father's many enterprises. In their blue house next door to the Edwardses, the Dwights had wallpaper embossed with velvet figures, and an elegant oak-paneled mantle. They were prosperous enough to have treated as a good joke on themselves a blunder they had made the first time they served tea. They did not know how to prepare it, so they steeped the whole precious quater pound at once, making a bitter brew that had to be thrown out.

The town liked to tell about the time young Timothy had played a trick on a notoriously absentminded farmer who was walking through the village beside a pair of oxen, occasionally flicking his team with a long switch to guide them. Timothy crept up behind the cart and held it with his bare hands, stopping the puzzled oxen. The farmer dreamily plodded on until one spectator yelled at him "Where are your oxen?" Another time Timothy won a lottery and refused to claim the money because after he had acquired the tickets, the Massachusetts law concerning lotteries had changed. Once a bully from a nearby town swaggered up to challenge Dwight to a contest. He found Dwight hoeing corn. Leaning on the fence by the garden, the visitor drawled, "They say you are the strongest man in town. I have come here on purpose to try my hand with you." Dwight answered quietly, "I wouldn't want to hurt you," and went on hoeing. The man continued to twit him. Finally, Dwight reached over the fence, picked up the visitor, whirled him overhead and nonchalantly deposited him back on the other side of the fence. Such a man follows his own heart, not popular opinion. So Dwight stoutly went on visiting Mary.

She was an extraordinary girl. Her father had trained her in the classics far beyond the level most girls of the time aspired to reach. She read voraciously, and was highly informed in history and geography. An old lady who knew her well reminisced that her "striking mental traits were her quick habits of observation and her thorough and keen analysis of men and things." Mary was blunt and impulsive—another neighbor recalls a story told of how he cried all day when he was a tiny baby because he was being weaned, and Mary Dwight shot out of her own house, marched into his home, picked him up and demanded of his mother, "Mrs. Tappan, what in the world is the matter with this child?" Some accounts say Mary Dwight had eight children, others say thirteen. Probably some stillborn babies account for the discrepancy. Among her descendants were two presidents of Yale and many other towering personalities of unusual physical handsomeness, so this was a romance with many consequences for society. But the engagements of the two daughters were the only glints of color in a gray year.

In the period from 1744 to 1748 not one new member had applied to join the church. Many townspeople had stopped speaking to any of the Edwardses. What the boys went through at school can be imagined. Edwards had believed that the role of the minister was to be a prophet, but the people disliked being made uneasy. They were tired of hearing from him about "the awful majesty of God." Edwards was simply too formidable a figure, and there was now no possibility for a reconciliation, though Sarah continued to try to bring one about.

While she was forced to lie down during her recovery from rheumatic fever, she composed a long letter in her husband's defense. She wanted to demonstrate that his stand on the matter of church membership had not been a highhanded impulse, but the product of sincere, slowly developed conviction. She tried to recall everything she could about the sequence of events, and she toiled over her report, correcting grammar and recopying it until it was much more polished than most of her writing products were. But she might as well have written in Swahili.

The political mood of the colonies that year added to the unhappy atmosphere. There was general irascibility because

1750 was a year of financial crisis. There had been no stable
hard money in the colonies since 1686 when the old pine-tree
shillings, in use since the 1600's, had been stopped. The states
began irresponsibly issuing paper money whenever they needed
cash. In April, 1740, the House of Commons tried to end this
financial anarchy. A long legal dispute followed between the
colonies and the British Government. Finally, in 1750 old
letters of credit were called in to be exchanged for Spanish
pieces of eight. Currency depreciated everywhere. Business
slumped. The prisons were jammed with debtors. One traveler
reported in June of that year that Boston was "as dull and still
as on Sunday." There was scarcely any money around except
a few copper pennies. There could not have been a less promising time for settling a quarrel.

Two hundred parish members signed a petition for Edwards' dismissal. This hurled the problem at the Hampshire
Association of Churches. Now came a test of the strong feelings both for and against Edwards which had been building up
among his fellow clergymen. The whole community around
Northampton was thrown "into a great turmoil."

Edwards recalled that the council was "a most disagreeable
and dreadful affair." Here Joseph Hawley enters our story. He
was the man mentioned earlier who though outwardly a substantial citizen was fundamentally unbalanced. At the council,
the Reverend David Hall of the town of Sutton tried to rally
Edwards' supporters, and he pleaded with the people of Northampton to remember "the former affection and harmony that
had long subsisted between them and their reverend pastor."
Joseph Hawley, sitting among the rustling spectators, shouted
Hall down.

Then Hawley seized the floor to read a diatribe against Edwards. Ten years later, in May of 1760, Hawley wrote an
astounding letter to David Hall. It showed that in all the years
between, Hawley had been haunted by the memory of the way
he had acted that day. He also sent a copy of the letter to a
Boston newspaper, where it was printed.

Referring to the way he had blocked Hall's effort to ask the people to act in charity, Hawley wrote to Hall:

> I heartily ask your forgiveness; and I think that we ought, instead of opposing an exhortation of that nature to have received it with all thankfulness. I with shame remember that I [acted] in a peremptory, decisive, vehement and very immodest manner. . . . But, sir, the most critical part of my conduct at that time . . . was my exhibiting at that Council a set of arguments in writing . . . which . . . contained some severe, uncharitable and groundless and slanderous imputations on Mr. Edwards, expressed in bitter language. And although the original draft thereof was not done by me, yet I foolishly and sinfully consented to copy it; and as agent for the Church to read it . . . which I could never have done if I had not had a wicked relish for perverse things. I now see that I was very much influenced by vast pride, self-sufficiency, ambition and vanity. . . . I had received many instances of his tenderness, goodness and generosity . . . the Church [was] guilty of a great sin for being willing to part with so faithful and godly a minister . . . because that was not generally known, I look upon myself obliged to take further steps, for while I kept silence, my bones waxed cold . . . your real, though very unworthy friend and obedient servant, Jos. Hawley.

Thus the true story of that June Sunday came out ten years later, after Edwards had been hurt all he could be and it was too late to spare pain to the family. At the time he wrote to David Hall, Hawley mentioned that he had sent a similar apology some years before in a letter to Edwards. Most men would have been tempted to rush into print with such a vindication. Edwards had not. Instead, he had written back quietly to Hawley:

> I have had enough of this Controversy and desire to have done with it. I have spent enough of the precious Time of my Life in it. . . . I am sir your Kingsman and Friend that

sincerely wishes your truest and greatest welfare and happiness.

But all this was to happen much later. On that actual dreadful day in 1750, Sarah and her husband had to sit in a meeting room where the very air crackled with hostility and listen while a livid Hawley spouted his vituperations.

When the council finally voted, the decision was 8 to 7 against Edwards. Two who voted against him were Chester Williams, of Hadley, and Robert Breck, the young man involved in the long-ago hassle over his ordination.

Hall found seven men to sign this statement by the minority:

> We cannot agree to the dismission of the Rev. Mr. Edwards . . . there is no just cause. . . . Because the church or at least its committee, while they offer us reasons . . . will not suffer us . . . to enter into the grounds of those reasons . . . which we esteem an imposition upon our consciences . . . we bear a free and cheerful testimony in favor of our dearly beloved brother . . . his praise is in most of our churches through the land.

One minister was so timid that he did not dare to vote either way. Edwards reminisced later:

> Two of the members of the council, who dissented from the result, yet did not sign the protestation viz. Mr. Reynolds and his delegate, which I suppose was owing to Mr. Reynolds' extraordinarily cautious and timorous temper.

So Reynolds, who was so solicitous about his own reputation, is now remembered because, on the one historic day of his uneventful life he was scared to stand up and be counted.

Hawley won that contest, but he spent the last twenty-four years of his life periodically sunk in melancholia. He continued to be a leading politician, and in 1766 was elected to the Stamp Act Congress, but he had periods of extreme depression. A contemporary reported that

he smoked incessantly on such occasions and his eye had
a wild and piercing look. . . . His friends . . . would
come to cheer him but rarely succeeded.

Hawley had no children, and willed his land to the town when
he died.

Crushed and repudiated, Edwards managed to make his
Farewell Sermon on July 2, 1750, a marvel of conciliatory
dignity. He did not come to this level of charity without soul
struggle. Notes left by Edwards show that he had long pondered
what he would say on his last Sunday, should he be dismissed.
At first he had blocked out a sermon based on a reproachful
text, Jer. 25:3, but he did not use it.

Sarah, sitting for the last time in the privileged seat where
she had known both exaltation and grief, knew how near the
controlled voice was to quavering as it spoke these words:

> It was three and twenty years, the 15th day of last Febru-
> ary, since I have laboured in the work of the ministry, in
> the relation of a pastor to this church . . . having always
> laboured under great infirmity of body, beside my in-
> sufficiency for so great a charge in other respects. Yet have
> I not spared my feeble strength but have exerted it.
> You are my witnesses that what strength I have had I
> have not neglected in idleness nor laid out in prosecuting
> worldly schemes and managing temporal affairs for the
> advancement of my outward estate and aggrandizing my-
> self and family; but have given myself to the work of
> ministry, laboring in it night and day. . . . But now . . .
> you have publicly rejected me and my opportunities cease.

While the stony faces stared back at him, Edwards continued:

> [Let us] consider of that time when we must meet one
> another before the chief Shepherd. When I must give an
> account of my stewardship; of the service I have done for
> and the treatment I have had among the people he sent
> me to, and you must give an account of your own conduct
> towards me . . . then it will appear whether . . . I have

been influenced from any regard to my own temporal interest, or honour, or any desire to appear wiser than others.

That was all he said in his own defense. Then he went on to tell of his hopes that the church could find a minister they could love and accept.

May you have a minister of greater knowledge of the word of God . . . and of greater skill . . . that such of you as have held fast deceit under my preaching may have your eyes opened by *his*.

Edwards then addressed special charges to five groups of people:

those who are professors of godliness
those who are in a christless, graceless condition
those who are under some awakenings
the young people
the children.

One of his admonitions gives a note of greatness to the sermon and provides a guideline for churches that may face similar upheavals:

Here I would particularly advise those that have adhered to me in the late controversy to watch over their spirits and avoid all bitterness.

Then the scrapper in Edwards could not, even in this lofty moment, resist a jab at his old enemy, Arminianism, the dilute, liberalized form of faith that, in his view, made goodness too easy.

The final moment had come. In a low voice, Edwards concluded:

Nothing remains but that I take my leave of you and bid you all farewell, wishing and praying to your prosperity. I would now commend your immortal souls to Him who formerly committed them to me. . . . May God bless you with a faithful pastor . . . and may you . . . during his life, and that a long life, be willing to rejoice in his light. And let me be remembered in the prayers of all God's

people that are of a calm spirit . . . And let us all remember, and never forget our future solemn meeting on
that great day of the Lord; the day of infallible decision,
and of the everlasting and unalterable sentence.

Those who walked home from that service, through the fragrance, the new green foliage of early summer, had an inti-
mation that, however much they hated him, a great man had
delivered a great sermon on July 2, 1750.

After disaster one must still face the next morning and in
going about the familiar motions one begins to live again. You
wash your face, heat water, gradually awaken, nerve by nerve.
In such small homely motions the body finds strength to go on,
then healing begins. So, in the first days of aftermath, Edwards
tore into his cluttered desk to whittle down piles of unanswered
letters that had come in during the crisis. He wrote to Erskine
and McCulloch in Scotland to thank them for their "letters
and presents." His prowling mind already had a new interest,
for he included in many of those letters an enthusiastic digression about the new college being started down in New
Jersey. The state's powerful governor, Jonathan Belcher, had
begun correspondence with Edwards about this project and
many of the planners welcomed his counsel.

Sarah probably did a delayed spring cleaning. In time of
emergency one doesn't notice dust on chair rungs, so her way
of swimming back to the surface of life again may have been
the way of any woman: hanging woolen blankets out to swing
in the sun and setting small boys to picking beans.

How to maintain the household was a pressing problem. Edwards' letter to Erskine ended with these lines:

I am now . . . thrown upon the wide ocean of the
world and know not what will become of me, and my
numerous and chargeable family. . . . I am fitted for no
other Business but study. I should make a poor hand at
getting a living by any secular employment.

The Princes in Boston rallied around and worked up a market
for fans and laces, which they encouraged Sarah and the girls

to make from scraps. Sarah, still dragging around after her bout with rheumatic fever, had to use all her ingenuity to stretch the slim funds they had for running the house. Scottish friends sent a generous collection, but last year's dresses had to be refurbished, every scrap of food stretched. All the family concentrated on making the house attractive to a buyer, for that was their one hope for revenue.

If Edwards had been willing to leave his denomination, many opportunities were open to him. A Presbyterian church in Virginia was so anxious to get him that they sent an agent all the way to New England to make him "a handsome offer." The new college in New Jersey angled for him to be president. If he had gone abroad, he would have been lionized. But he felt that his vocation was still to be a Congregational pastor in New England, which he continued to regard as an experiment in bringing the Holy Commonwealth into human affairs.

The unpleasantness at Northampton had been discussed throughout the colonies and all over the British Isles and the ripples of it carried far. One result was the first crack in the system of public support for churches, until then a custom throughout Western Christendom. Chileab Smith, great-grandfather of Mary Lyon, the founder of Mount Holyoke College, strongly supported Edwards. Because the church in South Hadley where Smith lived had opposed Edwards, Mr. Smith refused to pay tithes to that church. He moved to a new settlement and started clearing wilderness. The fields and fine orchard that he had left behind in South Hadley were confiscated to pay for the tithes he had renounced. Smith and his sons contested this. The case took ten years to settle, but finally the General Court in Boston decided in favor of Smith. This set a precedent which opened the way for the historic separation of church and state in 1834.

During that slow summer Edwards composed a farewell letter to the people of the parish. He signed the first draft "He who was your once affectionate and I hope through grace faithful pastor." When he reread the draft, he firmly crossed out "affectionate." While the Edwardses waited for someone to buy their house, the church in Northampton searched for a new minister. Both were slow and sticky procedures.

By rowing publicly with so conspicuous a figure as Edwards, the church had made itself notorious. Though the salary it dangled was the largest in New England, except for the Boston churches, other candidates were skittish about getting into the situation. Not only did the committee find it difficult to persuade a man to come permanently, they even found it hard to supply the pulpit with interim preachers. Edwards wrote a friend:

> The committee that have the care of supplying the pulpit have asked me to preach . . . only because they could not get the pulpit supplied otherwise; and they have asked me only from Sabbath to Sabbath.

The Edwardses had to go through an almost comic limbo when they were not free to leave, yet to linger was awkward for everyone. The church realized the incongruity of using Edwards as a substitute in the pulpit, so they gave up having preaching altogether to avoid using him. Hopkins says of Edwards' behavior in these hard months: "The calm sedateness of his mind, his meekness and humility . . . his resolution and steady conduct . . . were truly wonderful."

There was one cheerful day in the glum year. On November 8, 1750, Mary was married to young Timothy Dwight. A shaky Edwards, his emotions still close to the surface, witnessed the ceremony performed by Timothy's father, a judge. Then Mary moved next door and spent her life in Northampton. She never could bring herself to forgive the church for its treatment of her father, so she continued to attend services but would not go inside. She would sit in the vestibule on a chair beside the place where the bellringer stood to pull the chimes. On Communion Sundays, rather than share in the Sacrament with people from Northampton, fiery Mary Dwight rode twelve miles to share the precious service with people in a different parish.

Colonel Dwight offered to share half his income with Edwards if he would stay on as pastor to the families who had adhered to him. Edwards turned down this offer, though he found it touching, for he did not wish to split the congregation. The church, the gathered followers of God's will, was in his view still much more important than one man's hurt feelings.

The house did not sell and a new job did not open. Sarah stopped using white sugar and employed every imaginable way of using home-grown produce to feed the family. Then more personal abuse was heaped upon their financial anxieties. Hawley continued to connive against them. Later he was to express his regret that he published what he himself described in retrospect as "an unChristian, a scandalous, abusive and injurious libel against Mr. Edwards . . . for which I am heartily sorry and ashamed." Though Hawley's accusation was a flimsy contrivance based on his sick fantasies, it caused Edwards the humiliation of a public "remonstrance."

Finally, that fall, their old friend Hopkins maneuvered a call for Edwards to go as missionary to the Indians of Stockbridge, on the frontier. It was strange casting for Edwards, but this unpromising move was to prove delightful for the children, and the occasion for Edwards' greatest creative works of the mind.

# XII

## A Season of Harvest
## and Respite

They spoke no more of the small news of the Shire far
away, nor of the dark shadows and perils that had en-
compassed them, but of the fair things they had seen in the
world together.

—*J. R. R. Tolkien*

In her characteristic flamboyant prose style, Esther wrote:
"Among the bitterest of our experiences . . . was to be sent
roofless . . . into the wilderness, but neither my honored
mother nor any of the children bated a jot of hope." Though
their assignment in Stockbridge was opaque, and the memory
of the Northampton bruises still ached, the beauty of their
new setting began a convalescence for the whole family. Their
move was to a settlement in the glorious Berkshire Mountains.
It bordered the Housatonic River, so clear that the patterns of
twigs, pebbles, and ridged sand showed distinctly on its bottom.
Here taut nerves unkinked, spirits woke to joy again.

The area had first been probed by Major John Talcott in
pursuit of some mischievous Indians. Then Samuel Hopkins
had been one of a group who had negotiated with a chief of
the Mohican Indians to start a mission on that choice site. The
first missionary was a former Yale tutor, John Sergeant. His
commission differed from David Brainerd's, for Brainerd had
been a roaming evangelist while Sergeant was appointed to
settle in a single spot and build a parish. Timothy Woodbridge

was the village schoolmaster and the mainstay of the parish at the time the Edwardses arrived.

The land had been purchased from the Indians for £460, three barrels of cider, and thirty quarts of rum. That transaction turned out not to be a happy bargain for the tribe, who had the unfortunate Indian weakness for alcohol.* Four white families were installed at Stockbridge "to afford civilizing examples to the Indians," who were actually a gentle, domesticated tribe, chiefly interested in fishing.

The trail the Edwards family took in 1750 from Northampton to Stockbridge had not greatly improved since Benjamin Wadsworth, a president of Harvard, had described it in 1694:

> Ye road . . . was very woody, rocky, mountainous, swampy; extream bad riding it was . . . it has on each side some parcels of pleasant intervale land.

A road of sorts led down into Connecticut, where iron ore had been discovered in Salisbury in 1732. This mineral was described as "the richest this side of Sweden," and was highly prized for gun barrels, but in 1750, Parliament felt competition pinching the British iron forges and forbade America to produce iron. Left from the forty-five mines around Furnace Village (now Lakeville) was an access to the Hudson River. This made a window to the west for the Edwardses—a link with the middle colonies and the new college in New Jersey. This was to be a significant fact for Esther.

To the north was a forest so forbidding that Mrs. John Taylor, wife of the first settler who dared push up in that direction, "apprehensive from her seclusion that she should become unable to converse with her own sex, used to go out and

---

* In 1775 they sent a touching petition to an army officer: "We whose names are hereunto subscribed, being soldiers enlisted to serve in the provincial army during summer, beg leave to lay this request before you. We in our more serious hours reflect with shame upon our aptness to drink spiritous liquors to excess. . . . We therefore desire that . . . we may get so much as will be good for us and no more."

hold converse with the trees," according to local legend. The Berkshire winters were harsh. Edwards' contract stipulated that in addition to his salary of six pounds thirteen shillings, he be provided with eighty sleighloads of wood from the Indians and twenty from the white parishioners.

The General Court in Boston had chartered the mission, but money to run it came from British philanthropists, led by Isaac Hollis of London. There was a school of fifty-five Indian children, and a church congregation of several white families and forty-two Indians. Edwards could not speak the Indian language, so he had to lumber along with an interpreter as he preached. It was a strange employment for such a man, but it gave him the time and the tranquillity for the sustained thought he needed in order to do his writing.

Preaching to a stuffy roomful of these Indians was a rigorous assignment in winter because they covered themselves with bear grease as protection against cold. (They also used it to repel mosquitoes in summer.) But they loved to sing, and "the voices of the female Indians are particularly sweet and powerful." The women worked hard, raising maize and kidney beans with only wooden spades for tools, and making baskets and birch brooms. They aged early, dehydrated by work and childbearing, so a woman of Sarah's straight back and springy step was a wonder to them. Edwards wrote his father:

> My wife and children are well-pleased with our present situation. They like the place much better than they expected. Here, at present, we live in peace; which has of long time been an unusual thing with us. The Indians seem much pleased with my family, especially my wife.

The site of their house is now only a marker, a sundial on the lawn of an elegant sanitarium, but probably their home was similar to one still preserved which had belonged to John Sergeant, the earlier missionary. To pay for his new house, Edwards was forced to sell the land he owned back in Winchester, Massachusetts, where his father's people had originated. Turning to Timothy Dwight for help in unloading that property, Edwards explained that he was "in greater need of money than I expected." He had gone £2,000 (about $3,500) in debt during the bleak final months in Northampton. Giving "an outfit to two recently married daughters" had also sliced into his slim resources.

That first winter in Stockbridge, Sarah fell

> very dangerously sick, so as to be brought to the very brink
> of the grave . . . but [she had] an unshaken peace and
> joy in God,

according to Edwards. Betty, the sickly younger daughter, seems to have caught the same infection. Then daughter Sarah Parsons lost her first baby, Ebenezer. Grieving for that loss, young Sarah drooped, so Elihu Parsons bought a farm near Stockbridge, and moved, to let his bride be near the comfort of her parents.

In time the lovely surroundings and the simple kindliness of the Indians made all the family feel that in this new location they had reached a resting place. Edwards and Sarah began a habit of strolling to the spot where John Sergeant was buried near the Indian cemetery. The spot overlooked the winding river, the graceful hills and meadows, and while standing there reflectively, Edwards and Sarah began to be healed.

Edwards started to tunnel through a mammoth project that he had long dreamed about doing—a work on "Freedom of the Will." On Sundays, an Indian named David Naunakeekanuh blew a blast with a conch shell to bring the motley congregations to worship. If the people in Northampton had been stupefied by the erudition of Edwards, the Indians also must certainly have been. But they listened politely, sang with gusto, and were very generous to the Edwards family. When the first sturgeon appeared in the river and the Indians went out to catch them by torchlight, they would make a point of bringing back a fish for the preacher. They would set up summer wigwams in shady spots by the river and smoke the eels and sturgeon they brought back in their canoes. Some instinct for nutrition kept this tribe from scurvy, though they had no vegetables or fruit in the winter months. Their secret was the dried cranberries they kept to munch on through the winter. Furs were important status symbols to them, for the boldest hunter could flourish the most pelts. The smaller Edwards children found their new neighbors enchanting. In a short time they learned the Indians' language and spoke it as well and almost as often as they talked in English.

In January, 1752, Esther wrote this description of their new life to her friend back in Boston:

> This town is delightfully located for winter sports. The river has a very quiet flow so that we have skating parties and the hills all around furnish . . . coasting. I have just come in . . . with my cheeks all aglow and pulse beating wildly. My sister and I had two Indian boys pull our sleds for us and to guide them over the crust which flashes like a mirror as with lightning rapidity we speed. . . . At the corner the woodmen sped with their heavily loaded wood sleds and the sleigh bells rang out right merrily as tho it were a winter's holiday.

Another time she wrote:

> The chief place of social recreation and amusement is the singing school. Besides the pleasure of getting together the singers are permitted to set in the gallery on Sundays if they promise to keep to their own seats and not infringe on the women's pew.

For Edwards, one of the best aspects of the move was the proximity to his old friend Hopkins. Though Hopkins was often discouraged about his leaden parish at Great Barrington, where he had difficulty collecting his modest salary of £35 a year, he stayed there from 1743 to 1769. He often rode the seven miles to dinner with the Edwardses and long fireside talks.

Edwards continued to be a conscientious pastor to anyone who had to go through deep places, but his Indian friends did not expect a minister to make the conventional efforts to be

popular or to prod organizations. Thus the pressures that had
been on him before were eased. However, he could not bring
himself to write a book he had projected about the nature of
the church. That subject was still too painful.

For Sarah, these were ripening years. Her household still required sensible leadership, they still depended on the atmosphere
of love and gaiety she had a talent for supplying. But she had
passed the time of having to cut up meat for one toddler and
mop up milk spilled by another. The girls who had married had
made happy matches. The younger children either scrambled
contentedly about outdoors or when indoors amused themselves
by reading and handwork. So Sarah and Edwards had time
again for each other and the harvest of middle-aged love.

Enough has not been said about the beauty of love in the
middle years of life. By such a time in a marriage, the trying
habits of one's partner have either been accepted or are no
longer noticed, while the precious aspects of the other have
become so much part of the consciousness that they are like
leafprints stamped in stone. Memories, both of happy times and
of sorrow endured together, are glued into the marriage. The
ties between the two people are further fixed by the many years
of jokes shared and the common body of experiences. At this
stage in a relationship, to come back to the comfortable presence of the other after being out among many people is to be
rested and at home. All of this comes only after there has been
a profound tie of love. Without the love, the later years in
marriage can bring ennui.

As soon as she had the new house organized, Sarah began to
be hospitable again. Her invitations were particularly fortifying
to one lonely young man named Gideon Hawley. Hawley's
journal, which he kept from 1753 to 1808, repeatedly mentions
how good it seemed to him to return to the hospitality of
Sarah's house after the rigorous journeys he made as a missionary
to the Six Nations (Indians). Saturday, June 1, 1754, after
being "sick as death" in Cherry Valley Creek, he limply arrived at Stockbridge, and says:

I spent 13 days very agreeably at Mrs. Edwards in which time I saw Mr. Bellamy and other Friends which was very refreshing to me.

He went briefly back into the forest, but returned by July 10, when he picked up a copy of *Pamela* by Richardson, which he found in the Edwards living room. He "was exceedingly delighted with it—it is truly very instructive." He stayed to hear Edwards preach on John 10:27: "My sheep hear my voice, and I know them, and they follow me," and then he spent Monday still deep in *Pamela*. Hawley left at last on the seventeenth. It is not surprising that, after such a refreshing holiday, he wrote: "Set out on journey to Boston had some agreeable thots on road." By August 20 he was back in Stockbridge, filled the pulpit for Edwards, and stayed ten days.

He needed these respites, for his efforts among the Indians were discouraging. He analyzed the trouble:

> Lately Indians here have been very much afraid of English or white people settling here which they are very much against. . . . They are sensible of the grasping dispositions of white people.

When he returned to Stockbridge in April, 1755, Hawley found Sarah entertaining another guest, John Hamlin, but they warmly made room for Hawley and the next day Edwards, Hamlin, and Jonathan, Jr., Hawley's stoutest admirer and shadow among the children, rode a bit of the way into the forest with Hawley before he resumed his lonely journeys. He now had the Stockbridge habit chronically and he returned in August for ten more days.

His diary is in a joggled scrawl, as if he had written it while on horseback or before the unsteady light of a campfire. It reveals that this young man was more than a little a poet, and that he had a farsighted concept of the oneness of humanity. Here is a sample passage:

> Asked Chief to let me have a Path to his Town and if He ever saw me coming over the mountains he would not

I hoped shut a Door against me. I told him . . . the smoke
of our Fires mist together in the same air—we drank of the
same water and lived upon same food and therefore that
be glad we might in every respects [to] be one and spend
a happy immortality together.

It meant a great deal to this sensitive young man to have the
interludes in the warmth of Sarah Edwards' hospitality. They
offset the times of discouragement like the February day in
1756 when he wrote: "The week [aft?] I have done little for
God o how Time slides away and nothing done." So once more
Sarah, simply by being herself, affected the life of another.

Edwards rigged up a study in a closet 7 by 3 feet, where he
had a hexagonal table with inclining leaves so, as Esther described it, he "can have his books of reference before his eyes
all at once and can leave them open at the passage where he
leaves off." The chair he used is still at Princeton, with one
rung worn down as if he had propped one leg on it, to write
on a pad balanced on his knee. At last he could start on a book
he had described in October, 1748, but been "remarkably
hindered" in completing.

The result was *Freedom of the Will*, published in Boston in
1754. Proofreading this tome was so formidable a task that the
first printer confessed he gave only "a cursory review to these
sheets." Many snowy Stockbridge nights Sarah must have
brought out her knitting (to help keep her awake?) as her
husband read aloud to her the product of the day's skull-
cracking sessions in his study. It is a monumental work of
reasoning, though it has occasional human lapses such as
Edwards' habit of transmitting quotations loosely and changing
tenses if it suited him. He was still brooding about his humiliation at Northampton when he closed this work with the Bible
line:

God hath chosen the weak things of the world, to con-
found the things that are mighty . . . and the things
which are despised, hath God chosen.

From his hilly nook, Edwards also managed to be in the midst of a new enterprise in New Jersey, one that was to affect the Edwards family in a personal way, as well as to color the intellectual history of America. A new college had been formed, to be the voice of true religion in the colonies. It was younger and more religiously committed than the battered institutions in Cambridge and New Haven. Individual Scots contributed so enthusiastically to the project that the school was called "The Young Daughter of the Church of Scotland." The founding impetus for the school was an effort to spell out, in the training of human lives, the philosophy of which Edwards was the most prominent spokesman. The trail of the new college goes back to the Edwardses in other ways, for as one early president stated,

> If it had not been for the treatment received by Mr. Brainerd at Yale College, New Jersey College would never have been erected.

Everywhere, then, the wind was full of talk of new colleges. Franklin agitated for a university in Philadelphia in 1749:

> In the settling of new countries, the first care . . . must be to . . . secure the necessaries of life, this engrosses their attention and affords them little time to think of anything further . . . the culture of minds by the finer arts and sciences was necessarily postponed to times of more wealth and leisure . . . these times are come.

A similar notion led a group of men in New York to start King's College (later Columbia) with proceeds from the sale of ten thousand lottery tickets.

New Jersey was ripe for a school. By 1749 its population was described as "the most easie and happy people of any collony in North America." Prospering as a busy corridor for movement of products between New York and Philadelphia, the state was also fortunate because no powerful Indian tribes threatened its borders. The resident Indians were five thousand to eight thousand placid Lenapes, who had enough large woodlands to range so that they were contented and untroublesome. Because they

did not need to spend money on military defenses, New Jer-
seyans enjoyed delightfully low taxes. The Board of Trade
bragged in 1749 that " 'tis 17 years since any Tax was raised on
the people for the support of the government." The colony paid
its expenses almost entirely from interest on loans made to
settlers for improving their lands. There was a brief scuffle in
1755 when New Jersey and Connecticut disputed over one
northern parcel of land, and once in Essex County there was a
shady transaction in land which was sold two and three times
over, but in general life smiled on New Jersey.

The state was an oddity, culturally. West Jersey was influenced by Quaker Pennsylvania, while East Jersey was Dutch
and Scottish. The General Assembly recognized this cleavage
and alternately met at Perth Amboy, in the east, then at
Burlington in the western bogs. Even the currency reflected the
difference—a Spanish-milled dollar was worth more in the west
of the state than in the east. Happily fattening on the export
of meat and timber, the state could easily afford a luxury like
its own college.

The sedate Jersey Presbyterians had been scandalized by the
goings-on in other schools that they heard about. Harvard boys
were fined for climbing the college roofs and for stealing geese
from the town poultry yards, then roasting them over fires
in their rooms as a protest against the dull dining room meals.
Peaslee Collins, class of 1747, was fined for making "tumultuous
Noises," and when ordered to stand and be admonished he
"smiled and fleered in a most contemptuous manner." Yale was
just as rowdy, and it was reported that the college "shamefully
neglected" the study of Hebrew. In conversations over lunch
tables at Yale alumni gatherings, the friends of Edwards discussed the need for a school in New Jersey.

One of the planners was a short, cheery aristocrat, the son of
a judge in Fairfield, Connecticut. His name was Aaron Burr,
but he was not the notorious one of history. This Burr had been
a Yale classmate of David Brainerd, who had introduced him to
Edwards. He was independently rich and "had uncommon

powers in conversation . . . warm affections . . . was fair, open and honorable." One stout partisan of Burr was Judge William Livingston, member of the baronial family who had enormous holdings in New York and Vermont. The judge later became governor of New Jersey and the father-in-law of John Jay. Livingston had been in the same group at Yale as Burr and as he confessed, "I still seem to be in a rapture whenever I meet with a person whom I knew in College." As Livingston described Burr, "In him everything was agreeable, everything natural. . . . [He] inspired all around him with innocent cheerfulness."

Burr had been minister of the First Church in Newark, a town founded in 1666 by three boatloads of people who had left Connecticut, partly to get away from "the harsh east winds" and partly in pique because a royal charter had united the colonies of New Haven and Connecticut. They had bought from the Sagamore Indians an attractive site on the Passaic River, then a clear stream where children could skate in winter, canoe in summer. This transaction was so tactful that an old Indian said: "Not a drop of our blood have you spilled in battle—not an acre of our land have you taken without our consent." By 1716 the town had outgrown its first meetinghouse; when Burr came in 1736 he preached in a new 44-foot square stone building that was considered very grand for that day. The church's treasure was a sublimely fashioned baptismal bowl which the family of Deacon Azariah Crane had brought from England one hundred years earlier and used for bridal feasts before it was given to the church in 1730. The convivial Burr would have appreciated the bowl both as a symbol of celebration and of ceremony. The congregation were devoted to their dashing minister, and "through all his ministry there subsisted between them the most entire harmony."

When the new college was chartered, Burr enthusiastically voted for Jonathan Dickinson to be its first president. Dickinson, a leader of the synod, had been tutoring six boys in his church in neighboring Elizabeth Town, and these boys became the first class in the new college. Brainerd had come down to officiate at the wedding when in 1747 Dickinson, aged fifty-nine, was married to a girl of twenty-seven. But then Dickinson unexpectedly died after only four and a half months in his post as president. The trustees agreed with Livingston that Burr was "indeed most remarkably qualified for presiding over that grand undertaking," so he was unanimously chosen in November, 1748.

Burr's charm had even permeated the crusty Thomas Clap, who tried to entice him to First Church in New Haven because he was annoyed by Joseph Noyes, its minister. (Our plot thickens here. Noyes' wife was Sarah Edwards' stepsister, the one daughter James Pierrepont had produced by his second wife; after her death he had married Mary Hooker, Sarah's mother.) Clap tried to have Noyes removed on heresy charges, but Noyes had replied, "I am too old to be catechized" and simply refused to attend hearings. The Yale Corporation decided to "let Mr. Noyes die in peace and a member of the Corporation to his death."

One of Burr's favorite phrases was "vital piety." It was said that he "verily shone like a star" in the pulpit, and his faith carried over into his daily actions. A genuinely modest man, he wrote William Foxcroft, who had congratulated him about an honor he received, "I am bowed down under a Sense of my Insufficiency for ye important Trust." (Burr sent a barrel of flowers to Mrs. Foxcroft after a visit in their home. It was a gesture typical of Burr's graceful generosity, for Foxcroft was a rather lowly member of the Boston clergy hierarchy.) This affable man could also use a political stiletto, as he proved in the case of Robert Morris. In 1745 and 1746 there had been riots in Elizabeth Town when the East Jersey proprietors claimed land which certain settlers insisted they had previously bought from the Indians. When one of the defiant settlers was jailed for cutting timber on land he claimed was his own, his neighbors broke into the jail and released him. Burr openly sympathized with these rioters, whereupon Robert Morris, a leader of the proprietors, became Burr's opponent. In 1749, Burr learned that

Morris had gone to London to wangle an appointment as governor of New Jersey. Burr quickly warned his British friend, Doddridge, "Chief Justice Morris . . . tho a man of great Ingenuity . . . is (*sub rosa*) of most abandoned Principles."

Pouring out his energy to put the college on its feet, Burr accepted no salary for three years while he was making "long and tedious journeys, now ferrying over broad rivers, now riding through forests, now exposed to rain or snow, now splashing along muddy roads, to solicit funds for the college." He was a superb teacher. As one of his faculty said, "He had the most engaging methods of Instruction, set the most intricate points in the clearest light." In 1752, Burr decided to go abroad to raise funds. Edwards admonished him to get "a smallpox Inoculation before you go." (Vaccination was then a hotly debated innovation.) When Burr received that letter, he paused in his packing and reflected about his life's direction.

He was thirty-seven years old and the most eligible bachelor in the colony. Many hostesses had cunningly contrived to seat a niece next to Burr at a dinner party or suggested that the daughter of the house show him the view at sunset from the grape arbor. Burr had been absorbed in the infant college but he had remained single for more than academic reasons. The thought of Esther Edwards pursued him.

When Burr had last seen her, Esther had been the same age as her mother had been when first she attracted Edwards. Not only was Esther enchanting to view, she had "a peculiar smartness in her make and temper." She had qualities to be a consummate wife for a college president. She could reassure the shyest freshman, converse wittily with an arrogant faculty intellectual, make a trustee purr. Burr had been a guest in many elegant houses but at the Edwardses' he sensed an ambience that he coveted for his own household. A girl like Esther was worth waiting for, and now she was nineteen. Burr decided to send two deputies to Europe while he cantered up to Stockbridge on his handsome hunter, Nimrod.

The Edwardses were accustomed to having beaux about their

premises. Hopkins reported that "if any gentleman desired acquaintance with his daughters, after handsomely introducing himself, by properly consulting the parents, he was allowed all proper opportunity for it; a room and fire, if needed." For such a beau as this one, we can be sure that the smaller children were extracted from the scene and the visitor given every opportunity to be alone with Esther. In three days they were engaged.

Because Burr was heaped with work, the Edwardses made a decision so magnanimous that it was called "eccentric." In that time, weddings of the socially prominent were always held in the bride's house. Yet the Edwardses agreed to let Esther and her mother go down to Newark for the ceremony. Burr sent up one of his recent graduates to escort them, and the three set off, leaving Edwards at home to cope with the small children. First they took a trail to the Hudson River, a way so newly opened that workmen were still laying logs across squashy places and picking out stumps and stones. In the river valley were rich farmlands dominated by Dutch barns with pitched roofs as graceful as wings. At Albany, boats began the run to New York. As she skimmed past the Palisades, Sarah stared at the shore where her husband had gone hiking during his ministry in New York. ("I very frequently used to retire into a solitary place on the banks of Hudson's river at some distance from the city . . . and had many sweet hours there.") On June 29, 1752, Sarah sat alone, feeling the absence of the rest of her family, as a shining Esther was married to Aaron Burr.

The students collected coins to buy the bride "a silver can." These young men took a keen interest in the bride of their president. One wrote home to his parents, "I think her a person of great beauty, though I must say that in my opinion she is rather young (being only twenty-one [?] years of age) for the president." The young man's next letter home shows that Esther had melted him. He wrote: "I am sure when he was in the condition of celibacy the pleasure of his life bore no comparison to that he now possesses. I think her a woman of very good sense, of a genteel and virtuous education, amiable in her person, of great affability, very excellent economist."

Burr commissioned a painter to do twin portraits of himself and his bride. The paintings have quite a history. They vanished after some deaths in the family. Then Judge Ogden Edwards, Timothy's son, heard that they had been given to a servant named Keaser. Strolling one day on Pearl Street in New York, Judge Edwards heard a storekeeper shout: "Keaser, come here with your cart and take these boxes." The judge nabbed the drayman as he drove up, and learned that the paintings were with the man's older sister. She turned out to be living in a bedraggled shack in Millburn, New Jersey. The portraits were in the attic, stuffing a hole in the roof through which sleet and wind had poured. The judge bought the paintings, they were exhibited in a Philadelphia museum to general acclaim, but now have disappeared again. Many curators would like to know where they are because there is a strong possibility that the painter was John Singleton Copley.

After the departure of its most vivid member, the Edwards house in Stockbridge was a paler place. But there were two pleasant diversions for Sarah that year. On May 29, Sarah Parsons had a little girl whom she named Esther. In Northampton, on May 14, Mary Dwight had produced a son. These two babies were the reasons why Esther's sisters had been unable to share in her wedding. Mary's son was a prodigy. By the time he was eight years old, he had already prepared to go to college. By the time he finally went down to Yale at the venerable age of thirteen, he had covered the first two years of college work, studying at home with his mother.

People felt about young Timothy Dwight as vehemently as they had toward Edwards. He was so scintillating as a tutor at Yale that friends pushed him as a candidate for the college presidency when he was only twenty-six. Ezra Stiles was chosen that time, but after Stiles's death in 1795, Dwight was elected president of Yale, and gave the college a vibrant time until 1817. He introduced a new subject: belles lettres, started the divinity school and the medical school, and a chemistry department. In 1796 he preached a series of chapel sermons that blasted New England into another Awakening. (By 1802, a third of the boys at Yale claimed to be converted.) Dwight also managed to be an expert in church music, and to spark the founding of the foreign mission enterprise in this country, as one of the first Commissioners of the Congregational Board for Foreign Missions. One of the clues to his energy is in his phrase, which Mary Lyon loved to quote to her girls at Mount Holyoke: "One hour's sleep before midnight is worth two after."

Ezra Stiles actively disliked Dwight. He snorted that Dwight "meditates great Things and nothing but great Things will serve him." Stiles went through all his papers, fiercely erasing the places that mentioned Dwight. When later Stiles's daughter came into Dwight's office, she was indignant to find her father's papers stuffed into a cabinet with a broken hinge. A man of vast vitality, Dwight was a puzzling paradox, who had the courage to oppose slavery yet strained for public approval. He confessed once: "Particularly I have coveted Reputation, and influence, to a degree which I am unable to justify."

By December, 1753, Sarah Parsons had another baby, a boy called Elihu, and Sarah Edwards had a new career, as a grandmother presiding over the arrival of babies. Edwards muttered about how often she took off to help on these occasions. When Mary became pregnant again, Lucy wrote: "Who shall come, Mother or I? My father will not be willing if she stays a great while."

Edwards still needed his wife. He was wrestling now with the book that was to appear in 1758 as *The Great Christian Doctrine of Original Sin Defended*. When Edwards wasn't at work on his book, he wrote letters. Often he made duplicate copies in case one letter should be lost in ocean travel. To Erskine, August 3, 1757, he explained:

> Looking on these letters as of special importance I send duplicates, lest one copy should fail. The pacquet in which I enclose this, I cover to Mr. Gillies and send to Boston.

. . . I have reserved a copy of this letter and also of my other to you, dated July 25, intending to send them to Mr. Burr, to be by him conveyed by way of N. Y. or Philadelphia.

These were long, intricate letters, and the mind glazes at the thought of the work it meant to copy them twice in longhand.

As the quiet Stockbridge years ticked on, Sarah continued to be a hostess. John Wright, a young Scot who had been a favorite student of Burr's at Princeton, came for a long visit before he departed for England. Many young men continued to appreciate Sarah Edwards as a superlative hostess, though she was now in the process of accepting the fact of aging. For a woman who has been a sprightly belle to pass the irrevocable forty-fifth birthday is as drastic a time as adolescence is. As girls moving into their teens must get used to their unfamiliar height, their odd glandular impulses, their emerging features and gifts, so a woman as she shades into middle age has to accept a new self. She finds she has a changed level of energy, and is no longer eager to take chilly swims after sunset or whirl through three sets in a square dance. She finds ways to conserve her depleted resources. Sarah, who was totally feminine, had to meet all these implications of growing older, but Edwards gives no hint that he ever saw anything but the radiant girl he had married in 1727.

Their parallel roles—his to write, hers to sew and listen to him—are mirrored in a letter Edwards sent on August 27, 1753, to a Mr. John Ely of Springfield, Massachusetts.

Please to send us by Deac. Brown five or six yards of towcloth and also 5 or 6 yards of check that which is good and serviceable and reasonable and if you have any good Paper send me a Couple of Quire. . . . P.S. Please also to send 3 sets of knitting needles of the common size.

The tranquil days in Stockbridge were rumpled by a passing ruckus in 1753, when Edwards' moral plumb line got him into another feud. A fire in the Indian boys' dormitory made him uneasy, for it hinted of arson. This set Edwards to scrutinizing the affairs of the school, and it became clear to him that peculiar things were going on in its administration. He had become skittish about controversy, and at first determined to stay out of this matter. But he could see that the widow of the excellent missionary, John Sergeant, had not continued with the integrity of her husband. She had remarried, and along with her second husband was buttering an estate with funds that had been donated for work among the Indians. A conspicuously pretty girl, Abigail Sergeant had infatuated Ezra Stiles when he had visited Stockbridge in 1750. Edwards might have been scared away from his plan to move there if he had ever seen a letter Mrs. Sergeant had written to Stiles on November 6, 1750:

> Our worthy Deacon is going forth with to push Mr. Edwards Imediatly into the mission, all though he has Ben Intreated sufficiently to forbear. My father Captain Kellogg Mr. Jones & c are very bitterly against it.

From the start, though Edwards fortunately did not know it, he was unwelcome to the most prosperous white settler in the community, and to his daughter. She had been raised near Boston and kept her city tastes, so she refused to live among Indians on the main street. Sergeant had built a house for her on a hill above town. Still preserved, and now moved back nearer the center of the village, it is a handsome building, more substantial than a missionary might be expected to have. It has an elegant doorway, indoor paneling of burnished pine, and a bright, cheerful interior. Abigail saw that she was well equipped. The unworldly Edwards was no match for a woman as wily as she. Brainerd had not taken to her at all. He reported of a visit in her home that it was "spent in company and conversation which were unprofitable." The idealistic Timothy Woodbridge, the schoolmaster, and the deacon who had gone to try to persuade Edwards to come, had always mistrusted Abigail, but everyone had admired Sergeant and put up with Abigail for his sake until he died in 1747.

Edwards had no appetite for another fracas, but he finally decided to challenge the misuse of funds. Abigail had charge of the boarding school for female Indians, and her new spouse had the concession to supply all the equipment for the schools from his shop. Their personal servants were paid out of mission funds. Another member of the family was employed as an "usher"; four of their children had a free education there. A new building was to be placed on Abigail's land, and she was to be well paid for that. A New York merchant had received money for two years for "clothes for Indian boys," yet no Indian children appeared to be wearing those clothes. At last Edwards sent Timothy to Boston on September 15, 1755, with a letter to Thomas Prince, asking to bring the attention of the sponsors to this seamy situation. (Edwards wrote that he couldn't go along with Timothy because "two of my children are ill.")

Abigail's father was furious. He tried lobbying with the board of sponsors and Edwards wrote: "Captain Ephraim [Williams] is in Concord constantly busy with the representatives with his lime juice, punch and wine." The committee was unimpressed by the lobbying, and chose to take the word of Edwards. The Indians also confirmed Edwards' testimony. Once again the convivial Sarah had to face being snubbed in a small town by a lady who flounced off in the other direction when she saw an Edwards coming. Even Esther, safely married and out of it, wrote of her dismay at the "rupture." It is not easy to be married to a man whose conscience leads him into sticky issues. Edwards wrote to Erskine that "the business of the Indian mission since I have been here has been attended with strange embarassments such as I never could have expected."

Aside from the local problems, 1753 was so torpid a year that fifteen towns were fined for failing to send a representative to the state Assembly. There had been no issues live enough to stir a town to send delegates to these meetings, which granted lands, appointed officials, and made state laws. However, that year Edwards felt stirred to make his will because, as he put it, there was "much to make me sensible of the great Uncertainty of my life." So in March he drew up two and one half pages of close writing, which left Sarah his estate, as well as responsibility for deciding whether the boys should be "brought up to learning or to some Trade." Each boy was allotted 638 ounces of silver, which Sarah was authorized to dole out according to a schedule, depending on whether they were in college or apprenticed to a physician, a tradesman, or a lawyer. Edwards also provided for the "possibility that they or any or either of them should be sent Abroad." To the child who earned a "First degree at College," he dangled his library as prize.

The girls each received a half portion of silver, except for the delicate Elizabeth who still carried the mark of the anxiety Sarah had felt during that pregnancy at the time of Jerusha's death. Elizabeth, he feared, might have medical expenses or not be able to marry, so he willed her a son's share. To Sarah, Edwards entrusted his most precious legacy and his life's achievement—all his manuscripts.

In April, Timothy departed to study with Burr, though he was only fourteen. This was not an unusual age for a boy to go to college then. He could be admitted if he could pass an oral examination in Latin and Greek. Then he had to write out a copy of the college laws, the president signed it, and that served as his official permission to enter college. On the way down, Timothy was exposed to smallpox, and stopped in New York with a violent fever. It was a tense period for his parents, but he recovered. When he joined Esther, she was delighted to have a brother near. She wrote Lucy: "You don't know how smart Timo. looks with his new . . . coat. I think there is not one in college looks so smart and genteel." Soon Timothy decided he wanted to prove himself on his own, instead of being tagged as the president's relative. So he moved into the dormitory, to Esther's mortification.

> He had said nothing about it to me but only in general. When Mr. Burr was gone what if he should, what should I think of it should I be displeased and so on. . . . I promised my mother when she was here I would not op-

pose it . . . she said she thought it best I should not, but only think of it *No Brother!* . . . I expect it will set all the Town a talking, tis a pity.

Again, Sarah had her own way of handling a child. Though it embarrassed his sister, Timothy needed a chance to make his way on his own merits, and Sarah arranged for him to be free to make his own mistakes. Timothy, having had this chance to cut loose, ended by becoming a sedate citizen.

In 1754 the dozing colonies were jolted by the French and Indian War. France claimed the Ohio and Mississippi Valleys, which her voyageurs and priests had probed first. In France controlled the Midwest, the British coastal colonies might strangle. However, the British conducted this significant contest with stunning ineptitude. Lord Loudoun, commander in chief, wined and dined in New York City while Fort William Henry fell, and the Mohawk Valley, not far from Stockbridge, sizzled. William Livingston exclaimed that "there appears an Universal languor and Stupidity diffused throu[gh] the Plantations, and we sit Supine and inactive with the Enemy at our very doors." The coast was shredded by intercolony rivalries and by fights between governors and legislative bodies, though a few men like Livingston urged a unified war effort. Moreover, England had no notion of how to fight a guerrilla war, which was the French strategy. They used Indian tricks—ambush, deployment of scouts, conservation of ammunition—a form of war suited to the forest, whereas the British posted a few camps of mercenary soldiers along the borders and made gifts to the Indians, hoping to keep the Six Nations on their side. In 1756, General Braddock pushed out to what is now Pittsburgh and met a disaster. Even Gideon Hawley, who had been an expert woodsman, had found it grim to travel in the frontier wilderness. He once told of being "exceeding wet and not having any dry clothes was obliged to lay down wet as I was in an old dirty wigwam Indians had left and had but little quiet rest. The next day we met with showers again so we were obliged to ride with wet clothes all day." The clumsy British soldiers, used to the open fields of

England, found it hard going, and for a time it appeared that
the French would succeed in their plan to establish a series of
forts connecting the St. Lawrence and the Mississippi Rivers.

This ugly little war came close to Stockbridge in September,
1755, when there was a battle at Lake George with heavy losses,
and again in 1758 when Gen. James Abercromby met his disaster at Fort Ticonderoga. Their friends all worried about the
Edwardses. Joseph Bellamy, down in the safety of Bethlehem,
Connecticut, urged the whole family to come and stay with
him until the war was over. On December 3, 1755, Burr wrote
his friend William Hogg in England: "I have lately had a
Letter from Stockbridge. Mr. Edwards and his family are in
usual health except his daughter Betty who is never well & I
believe not long for this world—their situation is yet distressing
thro fear of the enemy."

Soldiers swarmed through Stockbridge and four were billeted
with Sarah. They ate so enthusiastically that she submitted a
bill to their commanding officer for eight hundred meals and
seven gallons of rum. Finally, Edwards wrote a plea that no more
such uninvited guests be tucked into their house. Sarah had all
she could manage to do, nursing Edwards for six months from
June, 1754, until the following January. He had a disagreeable illness which made him shake so he couldn't write—a form of tor-
ture calculated to make such a man a restless patient. To add to
Edwards' discomfiture, Sarah had to go help with the arrival of
another grandchild. Esther came up from Princeton to stay with
her father. She did not enjoy the jitters of war she felt all around
her, and wrote to a friend: "I am not willing to be butchered by
a barbarous enemy nor can't make myself willing."

Though Sarah and Jonathan stayed on in Stockbridge, they
did concede to the war to the extent of shipping away the
youngest children. Jonathan, a small, dark, plain nine-year-old,
took off to study the Indian language with Gideon Hawley.
"Pinty" and Betty went to Mary Dwight in Northampton. There
one afternoon Betty was trying to amuse her lively nephew,
four-year-old Timothy. She casually told him the alphabet, and

he seemed to enjoy it, so the next day she sat down with him, planning to review the letters. To her astonishment, the small boy recited the whole alphabet off to her. By the time he was five, he had raced through the Bible. He went off at six to the Northampton school where, when the bigger boys weren't using their Latin books, he would sneak a peek at them. By age seven, he had taught himself Latin. In another year he had siphoned up everything the local schools could teach him, but Mary felt that eight was really too young for Yale.

So she made a schoolroom in the nursery at home, fitting it up with desks and maps, and taught him herself, with stress on geography, history, and music. One way she kept him busy was by having him practice penmanship. He experimented with various makes of pens, grades of paper, and types of ink until he became a model of fine handwriting. Everything he could learn, he blotted up. Training a character to go with her son's phenomenal brain proved to be more of a problem for Mary. They told in Northampton how he once stole some pears from a neighbor's orchard and gleefully presented them to his mother as a gift. Mary made him return the fruit. The generous neighbor not only would not take the pears back, but the next day sent a bowlful over for the family table. Timothy was unable to eat them, for he was feeling stricken by his discovery of the lesson of the Eighth Commandment.

Back on the frontier, the war poked along. Two wayfarers killed an Indian in the woods near Stockbridge, and four people right in the town were killed by Canadian Indians. The fighting continued as a rumble in the background, and the war was not really resolved until the mighty battle in Montreal when both generals, Wolfe and Montcalm, were killed. The Edwards family, who feared God more than man, continued to carry on their domestic life, feeling less fear than their friends felt for them. It took a tragic twist of personal events, which came along next, to jolt them into an unforeseen change.

# XIII

## Two Presidencies
## at Princeton

Why should the aged eagle stretch its wings?
—*T. S. Eliot*

Though Esther Burr was lyric about her husband, and though many trips away from home had prepared her for absence from her family, she was surprised how much she missed them. "You can't write too often nor too long," she assured them. She missed the Stockbridge scenery but enjoyed an attractive two-story stone and frame parsonage where two brooks chuckled over rocky beds in the wide garden and pasture. Her husband encouraged her to pick up the study of Latin again, and the couple read Cicero together, with the help of a Latin textbook that Burr had written. Burr knew that the happiest diversion he could arrange for his bride was a visit from her father. So he set up an invitation for Edwards to address the combined Synod of New York and New Jersey. Esther was so much like her father that their two strong personalities had sometimes jousted, but she was devoted to him. Hers wasn't the only misty eye when the schooner swooping down from the north docked at Newark in September, 1752. Edwards paid for his trip with a long, tightly reasoned sermon on "True Grace Distinguished from the Experience of Devils." As on so many Sundays of her girlhood, Esther looked up at the tall figure, made even taller than its mortal six feet one inch by the exalted words of the peroration: "True religion is a divine light in the souls of the saints and as it shines out in conversation before men, it tends to induce others to glorify God."

When Esther had a baby, Sarah, the child had a "crooked neck." Struggling with her rebellion at this, Esther said, "Perhaps God foresaw yt we Should be too Proud of her." A letter she wrote home in 1754 gives a vivid view of the young mother. The writing is vigorous, so vivaciously underlined that it gives an effect as animated as conversation. "You will not wonder if you see many blunders for I write Rocking the cradle." Many blotches and crossed-out words confirm that she was being distracted.

Evidently Mary Dwight was pregnant again, for Esther goes on to say to Lucy:

> I am very glad you are with Sister Dwight at this time . . . as soon as [she] is abed contrive I should know it for I feel much concerned about it. I hope Mother will be with her. . . . I have no news to tell you I think. O yes! I have! . . . Mrs. Sergent* is like to have a child, pray what do you think of this? I know you will laugh.

Here there are several blotches on the paper and she explains them:

> Now I write with Sally in my arms for I am resolved to write. . . . I am exceeding glad to hear that Pinty [Pierpont] and Betty are at Northampton. I hope they will not go to Stockbridge til the danger is quite over. I wish I had some of em here with me, give my very kind love to em, tell em I think a great deal about them and long to see them. A deal of love to your self.

Probably Esther has had some tart comments to make on the frequencies of Mary's pregnancies, for she adds the admonition: "I tell you not to shew my letters to Mr. Dwight and you must tell me yt you will not." Then she impulsively inserts a scrap of extra paper with a postscript: "I had 6 sorts of flowers in the

---

* Esther's spelling was as atrocious as her mother's. This is probably a reference to the wife of Jonathan Sergeant, college treasurer.

garden . . . and in 2 days more should have pinks blown the
Second time. . . . The biggest part of people go to meeting
without their clokes yet."

On February 6, 1756, while her husband was out of town,
Esther was "unexpectedly" delivered of a son. She had, fortunately, a "very quick good time," though three weeks later she
had a mild setback. The baby was a puzzle from his first day.
Esther wrote that he was "a little, dirty, noisy boy . . . very
sly and mischievous . . . has more sprightliness than Sally . . .
handsomer, but not so good-tempered . . . very resolute and
requires a good governor to bring him to terms." This baby was
to be the clan's most infamous product, a complex character
who seemed to carry the family traits in some sort of Satanic
reverse.

## COLONEL B.

### By Constance Carrier

Eight lines of clergymen converged
to meet in Aaron Burr:
Edwardses, Tuthills, Pierreponts, each
a blood-and-thunderer
whose brimstone fire and sulphur smell
transfixed the listener.

Eight lines of clergymen converged,
as I have said, in Burr,
but Aaron was Beelzebub
in mocking miniature,
who cast Religion forth and had
no further truck with her.

So flatly contradictory
the parts of Aaron were,
not all of us can damn him quite
without some faint demur:
rascal and profligate indeed,
scholar and sophister

(that fox's profile, sharp and small),
the suave practitioner
of his own ethic, Arnold's man,
a brilliant officer
("—untrustworthy," said Washington,
unable to concur).

A Catiline, to whom young men
would eagerly defer,
corrupter of the innocent,
condemned a murderer,
chevalier, if not sans reproche,
past any doubt sans peur.

His daughter's idol, and his wife's—
the pictures blend and blur.
At eighty, unregenerate,
he died, in character:
"God's pardon?" "On that subject I
am coy," said Aaron Burr.

Because 1756 was a strenuous year for Esther, Burr arranged for her to have extra help. He bought from John Livingston, of New York, brother of his friend William Livingston, a Negro man named Caesar for £80. But he was unsuccessful in an attempt to give her the best present of all, the nearness of her parents. In 1755 he had hinted to William Hogg: "We hope by the help of some generous benefactor . . . to support a Professor of Divinity. The Trustees have their eyes upon Mr. Edwards and want nothing but ability to give him an immediate call to that office." Though Mr. Hogg was a stout admirer of Edwards, he evidently did not take this hint, for the professorship was not donated.

The college had outgrown its temporary quarters and it was clearly time for a move to a new campus. Edward Shippen recalled that "we had great struggles and long debates about location." Some trustees wanted to move to New Brunswick, but Princeton was reputed to be protected from New Jersey's notorious mosquitoes and was a natural stopping point between New York and Philadelphia. From Amboy Bay the Trenton Road arced twenty-eight miles to Princeton, past the ash swamp near Metuchen, past the widow Martin's tavern, de Peyster's house and mill on the Raritan River, past the farms of "Low Dutch personages" and a Dutch church. After a six-mile stretch of white oaks, maples, chestnuts, came John Manly's Tavern, then a string of sixteen farms and a meetinghouse which indicated that the traveler was nearing Princeton.

It was even then an attractive town. "Most of the houses are built of wood and are contiguous, so that there are gardens and pastures between them" wrote a 1749 visitor. Brainerd had spent his three best months working with Indians near there, reporting them "attentive, orderly and well disposed." By 1756 the town already had some elegant houses. The most imposing was owned by Richard Stockton on a 500-acre tract he had purchased from William Penn. The lovely house he built in 1701 had only shortly before been given the name Morven. The elegant ladies in 1755 were all reading *The Poems of Ossian*, in which there was an account of an ancient king, Fingal, of Caledonia (Scotland). This collection of epic poems probably was a literary hoax, but Annis Boudinot Stockton loved them and named her house after Fingal's castle. Morven, still a marvelous example of early American architecture, is now the residence of the governor of New Jersey.

Robert Smith, who was the inspired builder of Philadelphia's Carpenter's Hall and St. Peter's Church, designed the new structure at Princeton. Burr wanted to name it after Governor Jonathan Belcher who had been the king's representative in the state since 1747. Belcher's interest in the college was much more than official. He had presided over the meeting that elected Burr the president, and had become Burr's warm friend and supporter. Esther and her husband often visited the governor's mansion in Elizabeth Town, and Belcher once wrote to Burr: "You cannot be more thoughtful and solicitous for the growth and prosperity of my adopted daughter and our future alma mater than I am."

However, when Burr suggested to Belcher that his name go on the building, Belcher declined, with the graceful retort that he aspired to be "useful rather than conspicuous." The line is still used by one of the college's venerable social clubs as its motto. Instead, Belcher suggested naming the building for William III of the House of Nassau, who had "delivered the British nation from those two monstrous furies, Popery and Slavery." (Belcher may have been a gracious gentleman, but he was not ecumenical.)

Building Nassau Hall was as frustrating as such projects traditionally are, and it cost more than estimated. Burr wrote to a British donor: "The Building proves more expensive than we first imagined from the best computations we could get." The plan was to use the beautiful, mellow-hued native stone that is a characteristic of Pennsylvania houses, but Burr fretted about getting the stone, and wrote to Henry Cowell, a member of the Building Committee: "Let me know if you think I had best bring a man with me to Princeton that understands quarrying."

The carpenters poked along, Burr hovering anxiously over them. Finally, on the last possible day before snow fell and the winter term began, they moved in. Carpenters were still hammering on the unfinished basement. Burr had been determined to "do everything in the plainest and cheapest manner consistent with Decency and convenience." Using that criteria, he and Robert Smith managed to produce a building that has been considered one of the architectural gems of America.

Nassau Hall was supposed to house one hundred people— students and tutors stirred together. Behind it were two wells, an outhouse, a shed for a fire engine with leather buckets. On the east was a kitchen and the steward's quarters. A row of little buttonwood trees had just been planted nearby, but otherwise the scene was bald and raw when the students moved in.

Esther, meanwhile, was delightedly settling into the house Burr had built for her next door, largely from his own funds.

When the trustees tried to lure John Witherspoon to be their president in 1766, they dangled that house as bait:

> A large hansom and commodious Dwelling House is provided for the use of the President, together with a good garden and sufficient quantity of Land to furnish him winter fuel and Pasturage.

Still inhabited by the dean of the college today, the house Burr built for Esther was airy and attractive, with a nobly proportioned front hall. Along its wall there is still a long bench, where students once sat while they were waiting to see Burr.

There were two splendid living rooms, on a scale appropriate for the large amount of entertaining Esther pitched in to do, after the manner of her mother. In a darkish back parlor, Burr conducted faculty meetings, away from the noise of Nassau Hall. Upstairs were four bedrooms, one still containing a highboy with the initials "A. B." inlaid in the top middle drawer. In the kitchen was a huge fireplace, with a mantle over which a rifle could be hung, though even by the time of Esther that was an anachronism. Outside the brick doorstep of the kitchen she promptly planted a garden.

The hospitality that Esther inherited from her mother made her a shining asset as a college president's wife. She wrote home about having eight ministers for dinner on a Wednesday, ten the next day, followed by a supper for thirty-one guests.

Esther also had students living in her house, as the college enrollment soon spilled over its one dormitory. Everyone in the Burr house was aroused at a dark hour before dawn when a horn blurted out in Nassau Hall next door, summoning students to chapel at the merciless hour of 5 A.M. The chapel, lighted by candles, was as cold as a ship's deck in winter. Under a life-size portrait of Governor Belcher, students sat to hear prayers led from the high pulpit, morning and evening. They also returned to the same room to give declamations and read poetry aloud. The new college was soon clearly on its feet.

Though he might now have relaxed and enjoyed some of the

margin of his independent wealth, Burr continued working hard for the sake of his school. Edward Holyoke once remarked, "If any man wishes to be humbled or mortified, let him become President of Harvard College." Similarly, Burr was pushed to the last notch of his energies. As Esther once described it: "Company come and go come and go continually it is rap rap is the president at home all this day." In addition to serving as his own staff of deans, Burr also acted as college chaplain and superintendent of grounds.

Fund-raising continued to be a chore for him, though the college was off to a happy start. Burr had written to William Hogg about "the very agreeable news about the Scotland collection which has exceeded my expectations at least 300 pounds." He nevertheless continued to ply the British benefactors skillfully with such comments as: "We labor under Difficulties at present . . . for want of Books. We trust God in his Providence will raise up Benefactors."

On another occasion he wrote to the same friend, Mr. Doddridge, about a scheme he had for filling out the Princeton faculty with some British teachers. He sent the young son-in-law of the minister in the Presbyterian Church in New York City to scout about in England for them, and also added, "I am in Hopes he will be able to do Something for us by procuring some books or Mathematical Instruments which are much needed."

A happy facet of these fund-raising efforts was the fact that Gilbert Tennent, who had alarmed Edwards during the Awakening, had now settled into an irenic ministry in Philadelphia and was proving to be an effective fund raiser for the college on the side. Another triumph for Esther was the mollifying of Robert Morris, who seemed to be mellowing toward the college.

The students had a good time. A frequent entertainment was loitering at the tavern to watch the New York stage come flying in. They also organized hay rides to Trenton and when there was a Dutch wedding in the neighborhood, students joined in the "drinking and fiddling and dancing." Many of the all-male college students were as shy with girls as the Yale boys

who were, as William Livingston snorted, "struck dumb at the
sight of a spreading hoop or a lace waistcoat." But Esther's
brother Timothy was used to girls—he had many sisters and a
mother who was a social virtuoso, so he cooperated enthusiastically with Esther's matchmaking on his behalf. She had her
eye on Rhoda Ogden, of Elizabeth Town. Her father, owner of
a substantial section of "rich, level soil," had been Burr's friend
since the riots. Her brother was already showing the hearty
talents that were to make him a senator and governor, and a
confidante of Washington. Rhoda was bright, vivacious, and
kind, and when she was Esther's guest, Timothy was easily
persuaded to drop in.

The next year Burr wrote ominously to George Whitefield,
"The fatigue I have had in the care of the College this winter
has been greater than ever being obliged to do the duty of a
Tutor as well as my own, one of them being taken off from
duty by illness." In the sultry summer of 1757, Burr made a
hasty trip to Stockbridge to give Esther and the children a visit
with her family. On August 19 he whizzed back to plead with
the legislature that college students be exempted from military
service(!). Though he felt seedy on August 21, he went to
Newark to preach at the funeral of the tutor who had been
ailing. Then he scurried back to a mountain of desk work. His
bookkeeping listed: "David Hull 3.40 for tuition . . . 18s. for
Elizabeth Crane's horse . . . 14.33 for tutor." After making
plans for commencement and the trustees' dinner he dashed to
Philadelphia on college errands.

Next occurred the worst possible thing. Governor Belcher
died. The college lost its most powerful supporter, and Burr a
treasured friend. He felt obliged to preach the funeral sermon,
though by now he had an intermittent fever. He lashed himself
all day to write the sermon and rode to Elizabeth Town with a
sizzling fever. "When it was obvious to everyone that he ought
to have been confined to a sick bed he with great difficulty
preached the sermon." The following day he tottered into the
cool, shaded entrance hall of the house in Princeton and col-

lapsed. He died on September 24.

Esther was pulverized. She wrote to one friend: "Your most kind letter of condolence . . . set open afresh all the avenues of grief and again probed the deep wound death has given us. My loss—how shall I attempt to say how great my loss is. God only can know and to him alone would I carry my complaint. Indeed, sir, I have lost . . . all that ever I set my heart on in this world."

Sarah and Edwards were crushed to lose a cherished friend, and they suffered deeply for their daughter. Gradually the training they had given her supplied her with strength to meet the crisis. On October 7 she was able to write to her mother:

> God has seemed sensibly near, in such a supporting and comfortable manner that I think I have never experienced the like. . . . Thus dear madam, I have given you some broken hints of the exercises . . . of my mind. . . . O dear madam! I doubt not but I have your and my Honoured Father's prayers, daily, for me, but give me leave to entreat you to request earnestly of the Lord that I may never . . . faint under this his severe stroke. . . . O I am afraid I shall conduct myself so as to bring dishonour on . . . the religion which I profess.

Edwards wrote his daughter a reply typical of both his realism and the ways in which people found him exasperating in his clearheaded unsentimentality. "Don't be surprised, as tho' some strange thing had happened to you, if after this light, clouds of darkness should return." He loved her so much that he did not want to encourage Esther to think she had yet survived the full ordeal. Though her parents longed to make this time easier for her, they realized that she still had grief work to do and that no one else could assume it for her.

In time of extreme shock, one is carried along by reflexes. Crisis reveals what one has been trained to do by habit. So now the training Esther had received at home helped her to be busy about practical matters, in a saving therapy. She set about organizing Burr's accounts, and on November 17 wrote to their grocer:

> I find by Mr. Burr's Acc't Book yt all his acc'ts were Ballanced to March 29. Since that time I find these peticulars I now send you. I showed Mr. Baldwin your Letter. I suppose he will soon send the cash for the coffee and sugar.

Burr's will italicized the devotion he felt for all his wife's family. He left a £50 legacy for Elizabeth, the frail younger daughter. The settlement of his affairs also confirmed how generous a man he had been, for it turned out that many people owed him debts he had not pushed them to repay. His account books were sprinkled with such entries as a loan in 1756 to one student who found that the move from Newark to Princeton would be a financial hardship. Burr had advanced him money for the move, "for bringing his chest and expenses in going to Princeton." It was typical of his character that one of Burr's last words had been to ask for an "inexpensive" funeral and to request that the saving be given to charity. Burr also left money for his two children to be handsomely supported and educated. But his death took away the one thing his small son needed most—the firm hand of a loving father.

Burr had died on September 24, two days before commencement, the least convenient time for a college to lose a president. (It caused a personal dislocation for young Timothy Edwards, who had been scheduled to graduate then, and his great day was clouded by the family's grief.) The Princeton trustees scrambled about quickly to arrange for continuity of leadership. Obviously, Edwards was the man to hold the college together, but he was flabbergasted to be asked. He wrote back, on October 19:

> The chief difficulties in . . . the way of accepting this important and arduous office are two: First, my own defects, unfitting me for such an undertaking, many of which

are generally known; besides others of which my own heart
is conscious. . . . I am also deficient in some parts of
learning, particularly in algebra and the higher parts of
mathematics and in the Greek classics.

For many hours Sarah and Edwards debated the invitation.
Edwards had planned two ambitious study projects: a "History
of the Work of Redemption" and a "Harmony of the Old and
New Testaments." Should he stay in serene Stockbridge, which
suited his study habits so well? Tugged by these projects and
aware of the many public appearances required of a college
president, Edwards mused to Sarah, "I think I can write better
than I can speak."

On the other hand, Burr would have wanted this successor,
and surely Esther needed to have her parents near. Finally,
Edwards decided to accept, and replied:

I think the greatness of the affair and the regard due so
worthy and venerable a body . . . requires my taking the
matter into serious consideration.

The trustees read this to be encouragement for them to send
agents to Stockbridge, though it was in the midst of winter
weather. These men put before a church council the case for
Edwards' leaving. When the council decided it was Edwards'
duty to go, he astounded everyone by bursting into tears, "which
was very unusual for him, in the presence of others." Perhaps
he was overcome by the realization that at last, after so many
years of miscasting, he had come into a role he had always been
meant to hold.

Though her sister Lucy had gone to Princeton to stay with
Esther, she could scarcely wait for her parents to get down.
She was feeling overwhelmed by the responsibility of carrying
on alone with the two tiny children. Little Aaron had a fever,
and she had conniptions about that until she finally brought
herself to a point of being able to say "God showed me that
the children were not my own but his." Edwards, realizing the
burden she carried, wrote her on November 20:

Dear daughter: I thank you for your most comfortable letter but more especially I thank God that has granted you such things to write. How kind is your heavenly father. How do the bowels of his tender love and compassion appear, while he is correcting you by so great a shake of His Head!

Then he went on to mention his concern about whether he could afford "to furnish the House." He continued:

As to Lucy's homecoming her mother will greatly need her especially as we remove in the spring. But whether your circumstances don't much more loudly call for her continuance there must be left with you and her. . . . Your mother is very willing to leave Lucy's coming away wholly to you and her. I am your most tender and affectionate father.

Of course Sarah decided that Esther needed Lucy more, so Lucy stayed on in Princeton. Sarah supported Edwards completely in his decision, and in this she spared the trustees the suspense they were to have later with Mrs. Witherspoon. That lady was a quiet homebody, with many children, and she did not at all want to leave Scotland. Richard Stockton made an uncomfortable February trip to Scotland to try to persuade her; and one of his arguments with Mrs. Witherspoon was that Princeton was "the cheapest place in America"—a canny bait for a Scottish housewife. Benjamin Rush had to make another trip. Then followed a comedy of errors. By the time Witherspoon's wife was finally ready to move, the trustees had asked another man, Samuel Blair, to take the job. The exhausted trustees were stuck with two presidents. Fortunately, according to Stockton, "Mr. Blair was so much disgusted that he certainly would not come in."

Edwards told Esther he might not make it down to Princeton until spring, and she wrote back: "Perhaps I counted too much on the company and conversation of such a near and dear affectionate father and guide." This melted Sarah, and she persuaded Edwards to start down and leave the moving for her to manage later. She had Titus, "a Negro boy valued at 30 pounds" to help her, and Sukey was now old enough to be a delightful companion for her mother, so she convinced Edwards that Esther needed her father as soon as possible. He went down to be with her on February 16, 1758. His last Sunday in Stockbridge, Edwards preached on "We have no continuing city, therefore let us seek one to come," and he read from Acts, ch. 20. ("O how proper; what could he have done more," exclaimed Sukey.) When he got out of doors after the service, he was deeply moved by the parting and impulsively turned about to say from a full heart to the people clustered at the door, "I commit you to God."

Administrative work had heaped up since Burr's death, and Edwards settled down at Burr's desk to tunnel through the accumulated papers. He also began to conduct what would now be called "preceptorials," in which he gave out questions in theology to members of the senior class. They were to go off and dig out the answers on their own, then return to defend with Edwards the positions they had thought through. It was the kind of exercise Edwards had done with the young men who had trained with him for the ministry, and the students would have had an incomparable intellectual experience had Edwards been able to carry out the plan.

However, he had been at his desk only a week when he decided to have an inoculation against a smallpox epidemic that had begun to sweep into the state. It was like Edwards to take a chance on something still in the experimental state and hotly debated. The city of Boston had been torn apart by the subject in 1721, when a great plague had been brought into Boston by a Negro who came in on a ship from the Caribbean. More than half the city's population caught the disease. Cotton Mather had heard about inoculation, which was being used in Turkey, and he begged the doctors to try the idea. Only Zabdiel Boylston took the suggestion. He tested the vaccine on his own small son, and caused such a ruckus that he was mobbed in the street. Mather was angrily denounced, and a bomb was tossed at his house. When the epidemic was spent, and tempers cooled enough for a rational evaluation of the controversy, it was seen that of those inoculated the death rate was one in forty; while in others, the rate had been one in six. Many people still remained unconvinced, though Thomas Prince was one who came to support inoculations.

Edwards, always interested in science, had followed the subject. (We remember that he had urged Burr, six years before, to be sure to get an inoculation before he went abroad.) He reasoned that it would be good for the college if he set an example and had himself inoculated before the epidemic spread farther. President Holyoke had had to dismiss Harvard in May of 1752 because of an epidemic, and Edwards hoped to avoid a similar disruption, but his most compelling reason for doing this came out of the deepest part of his nature. He had written long before:

> Old men have seldom any advantage of new discoveries, because these are beside a way of thinking they have been long used to; resolved, therefore, if ever I live to years, that I will be impatient to hear the reasons of all pretended discoveries and receive them, if rational, how longsoever I have been used to another way of thinking.

Meanwhile, back in Stockbridge, Sarah was cheerfully packing china teacups and storing woolen mittens as she bustled about her packing for the move. Parliament had in 1752 changed the opening of the official calendar year to January 1, instead of March 1, which previously had been the first of the year in the colonies. One who has experienced "mud season" in New England understands why it had seemed to the early settlers that a new year did not really start until the long, locked-up winter season lifted. As soon as there was a respite from soggy spring thaws, Sarah planned to start out and make two stops on a meander to Princeton. She hoped to look in on a sister-in-law at West Springfield, and then to check on her mother-in-law in East Windsor, where the older Timothy

Edwards had just died at a great age. Though her children grumbled about leaving their beloved Berkshire hills, Sarah was sure it would be good for all of them to begin a new life in New Jersey.

Down in Princeton, new ribbons ominously appeared on doorknobs each day. That was the way people were warned to keep away from a house with smallpox in it. Watching the number of ribbons increase, Edwards decided to take the chance of inoculation. He wanted the best possible doctor to do it, so he persuaded Dr. William Shippen to come up from Philadelphia. Shippen was the first physician at the Pennsylvania Hospital. His brother Edward was a strong member of the board of trustees of the college. Both the Burrs and the Edwardses liked and trusted the Shippen brothers. Edwards felt that if any man was qualified to handle the tricky new medical procedure, William Shippen could.

On March 22, 1758, as spring had begun to slip into some Princeton gardens, and the cheerful yellow of forsythia flickered in a few hedges, Dr. Shippen sat down to write a difficult letter. It was to Sarah Edwards:

> Most dear and very worthy Madam, I am heartily sorry for the occasion of my writing to you, by this express, but I know you have been informed . . . that I was brought here to inoculate [your husband] and your dear daughter Esther, and her children, for the small pox, which was then spreading fast in Princeton; and that, after the most deliberate and serious consultation, with his nearest and most religious friends, he was accordingly inoculated . . . and although he had the small pox favorably, yet, having a number of them in the roof of his mouth and throat, he could not possibly swallow a sufficient quantity of drink, to keep off a secondary fever, which has proved too strong for his feeble frame; and this afternoon, between two and three o'clock, it pleased God to let him sleep. . . . And never did any mortal man more fully and clearly evidence the sincerity of all his professions, by one continued, universal, calm, cheerful resignation, and patient submission

to the divine will, through every stage of his disease, than he; not so much as one discontented expression, nor the least appearance of murmuring, through the whole. And never did any person expire with more perfect freedom from pain;—not so much as one distorted hair—but in the most proper sense of the words, he fell asleep. Death had certainly lost its sting, as to him. . . .

I conclude, with my heart prayer, dear Madam, that you may be enabled to look to that God, whose love and goodness you have experienced a thousand times, for direction and help, under this most afflictive dispensation of providence, and under every other difficulty, you may meet with here, in order to your being more perfectly fitted for the joys of heaven, hereafter.

I am, dear Madam, your most sympathizing and affectionate friend and very humble servant, William Shippen.

Sarah had asked herself whether she would ever be able to be resigned to the loss of Edwards or one of the children, and she had tried to be prepared for any testing life might require of her. Hopkins reports: "Her conduct, upon this occasion, was such as to excite the admiration of her friends; . . . she was sensible of the great loss . . . and at the same time showed that she was quiet and resigned, and had those invisible supports which enabled her to trust in God."

But her body betrayed how she felt. No amount of valor can prevent the body from reacting in proportion to the actual feelings. So Sarah acquired a thrumming pain. However, she managed to write this to Esther on April 3:

My very dear Child, What shall I say! A holy and good God has covered us with a dark cloud. O that we may kiss the rod and lay our hands upon our mouths! The Lord has done it. He has made me adore his goodness, that we had him so long. But my God lives; and he has my heart. O what a legacy my husband and your father has left us! We are given to God; and there I am and love to be. Your affectionate mother, Sarah Edwards.

To the same sheet of paper, Esther's younger sister, Susanna, attached a scribble which explained:

> My mother wrote this, with a great deal of pain in her neck which disabled her from writing any more. She thought you would be glad of these lines from her own hand.
>
> O sister, how many calls have we, one upon the back of another. O I beg your prayers, that we who are young in this family, may be awakened and excited to call more earnestly on God, that he would be our Father and friend forever.

Shock pounded upon shock. Dr. Shippen thought Esther was "safely over the disease," and for two weeks she appeared to be her usual incandescent self, though subdued by grief. Then on April 17, she had a sudden seizure and was gone.

Lucy had walked into immense responsibilities when she had come down to Princeton to help her sister. Now she carried on, trying to console the Burr children. The inoculation had taken lightly on the babies (little Sally had only three pox, on her face) but their world had disintegrated. Lucy was helped by the same college treasurer whose wife Esther had once joked about. Esther, who was as kind as she was impetuous, would have been stricken with remorse for her jocularity if she had known that the person who straightened out the Burr affairs now was Jonathan Sergeant. He ordered the rum and gloves for her funeral, paid doctor bills, sold Burr's wig, a small sheep, and a pair of turkeys, and arranged with Elihu Parsons about the finances of the Burr children. He proved a good neighbor.

Though she was dazed by her bereavements, Sarah decided she had to take over the care of Esther's children. By these monstrous circumstances she had again been given the vocation to be a mother. Perhaps beautiful Stockbridge would prove a restorative place for these battered children. It had been for Sarah's own children. Lucy undoubtedly needed relief from the responsibilities she had been carrying. So an emotionally drained Sarah started to Princeton.

In an effort to meet competition by a rival line the stage
wagons between Amboy and Trenton had spruced up, advertis-
ing that they were "fitted up with Benches and cover'd over
so that passengers may sit easy and dry." But even with these
refinements, the trip was a jouncy ordeal. To allow passengers
in rear seats to scramble across to their places, none of the
benches had backs. By the time she reached Princeton, thoroughly joggled, Sarah had concluded that the return would be
easier by boat. The water route took longer, but in 1750,
Robert Durham had introduced on the Delaware River a keel
boat shaped like an Indian canoe which might be easier traveling with two babies and lively eight-year-old Pinty.

Henry Cowell, minister of the Presbyterian Church in Trenton, was the trustee who had stepped in to run the college in
that interim. He was very kind. No one hurried Sarah in her
melancholy inventory as she moved through her daughter's
elegant house, sorting, dismantling, deciding what to carry to
Stockbridge to give the Burr children a sense of continuity
with their early years. What should she give away? What was
to be stored until the small Burrs were ready to furnish homes
of their own?

The house held poignant associations at every turn: the per-
ennials Esther had planted, curtains and towels she had stitched
as the family sat together in the evening by the fireplace back
in Stockbridge. Esther's dresses, even as they limply hung in
closets, seemed to stir with her special style. Edwards' familiar
handwriting leaped out at her from a desk drawer. The past
rushed back, yet it was gone.

The line of Scripture that had served as magnetic north for
the faith of Sarah Edwards was Rom. 8:35. "Who, then, can
separate us from the love of Christ?" The mighty confidence
of Paul supported Sarah now. The love she had shared with
Edwards had begun in the love of God, had been tinged with
transcendence for thirty-one years, had now returned to its
Source. The rest of that passage goes on:

> For I am sure that nothing can separate us from his love:
> neither death nor life; nor angels nor principalities; nor

things present nor things to come; nor powers; nor height nor depth nor anything else in all creation will be able to separate us from the love of God.

Her husband was safe and peaceful, she was sure, and so would she be. But after thirty-one years of a companion, of warm flesh to reach out to touch, an irrevocably empty bed makes the heart ache with solitude.

In the Princeton cemetery she visited three graves: Burr's, Esther's, Edwards'. A Latin inscription on Edwards' said, in part: "Do you ask, traveler, what manner of man he was? . . . The College weeps for his loss; the Church weeps; but Heaven rejoices in receiving him." What her thoughts were when she saw that marker, it would be impudent to speculate. But Sarah kept for her comfort the rich years she had shared with the man described on the stone. When Edwards had as a college student drawn up his list of seventy "Resolves," one had been: "Resolved, to live with all my might while I do live." He had done that, and she had been the chief reason he had.

She tried to compensate for the gay young mother the Burr children were sharply missing, and by the end of September, the packing was completed. Sarah was exhausted by the hard physical work of organizing a move, as well as by the emotional whipping of the past six months. Now that she was forty-nine years old it was harder to care for active toddlers. A dysentery epidemic hit her hard, and she had no strength to resist it.

Fortunately, the little troop had stopped over in Philadelphia. Gilbert Tennent's church contained old friends who could take them in and help with the care of the children. Philadelphia was then an enchanting city. A windmill marked the harbor which was always lively with shipping. (A single issue of the *Pennsylvania Gazette* for that year reported vessels clearing for Antigua, Jamaica, Barbados, Belfast, St. Christopher's.) Wide brick streets had a civilized pavement for foot travelers along each side. The State House (now Independence Hall) had finally been completed after almost twenty-five years of poky construction, and behind it was a delightful park. Dr. William Shippen and his family lived not far from there in an exquisite house with an unusual woody flowering vine in the garden. Some years later the Shippen home came into the possession of Dr. Caspar Wistar, who held open house for members of the American Philosophical Society and visiting scientists. The vine growing there was named wisteria in his honor. Beyond the town the land sloped up to Fairmount, where people went for picnics. There, Franklin had rigged up a battery-operated spit to amuse a party of friends—it was the first chicken to be barbecued on a rotisserie. But Sarah was not able to enjoy the charms of colonial Philadelphia.

After being for so many years the one who carried the burden when other people were sick, the one to tote trays and plump pillows, Sarah had to give in and let friends pamper her. For five days she was in such pain that she spoke little, but on October 2 she swam up out of agony and emerged into a kind of illumination. The instincts of a lifelong habit of orderliness led her to ask to draw her will.

She had been traveling with about £10 in money and personal clothing worth £13. She directed that her clothes be divided between her unmarried daughters, "share and share alike." The expression was typical of her. This had always been her approach to her children. As for the modest estate Edwards had left for her, she directed that its distribution be handled by her son Timothy and "my dear beloved son-in-law Timothy Dwight." Edwards' estate, again, was to be divided "share and share alike," but among all the children, married as well as single. Barely able to hold the pen, she signed the will in a wobbly hand.

With her were two witnesses, Valentine Standby and William Rowan. They reported that "she apprehended her death was near, when she expressed her entire resignation to God and her desire that he might be glorified in all things; and that she might be enabled to glorify him to the last; and continued in such a temper, calm and resigned, till she died." Again, it was Dr. William Shippen who had to sign this death certificate, and Samuel Hopkins was her devoted chronicler until the end.

So many deaths in so short a space of time give this narrative the aspect of the end of a Shakespearean tragedy where bodies strew a stage. Perhaps this is the only way a story like this could conclude with dignity. Some women do go on to find a second shell for themselves after they are widowed. Somehow they start again. But simple gallantry would not in Sarah's case have been enough. These had been two people bound together as few couples are. Now, still beautiful, she hastened to join her husband.

In the last minutes of his life, Edwards had tried to speak. Lucy, Esther, and Dr. Shippen leaned forward. Edwards spoke in a low voice and still distinctly. The words were not about heaven or hell, or about books or theories. He spoke of Sarah:

> Give my kindest love to my dear wife, and tell her that the uncommon union which has so long subsisted between us has been of such a nature as I trust is spiritual and therefore will continue forever.

# XIV

## "A Family Is a Kind of Gulf Stream"

> It was particularly affecting to me to think that the
> earth remained the same through all these changes upon
> the surface: the same spots of ground, the same mountains
> and valleys where those things were done, remaining just as
> they were, though the actors ceased.
>
> —*Jonathan Edwards*

In September, 1874, in "well-nigh perfect" weather, between
four hundred and five hundred descendants of Jonathan and
Sarah Edwards poured into the summer resort town of Stockbridge, Massachusetts, for a family reunion. They lunched
together in a huge tent Yale had loaned for the occasion, had
a picture taken of the whole throng in front of the Stockbridge
church, admired an exhibit of memorabilia which included
Sarah's wedding dress and the silver porringer from which Edwards used to eat the austere bread and milk that was his
favorite supper. The house where the Edwardses had lived on
Main Street was then "comparatively unchanged," so they all
peered and poked about it. The gathering teemed with professors, with successful business executives, with government
officials and clerics, and with women of unusual beauty and
force of personality. The mood of the reunion was expressed
by J. E. Woodbridge, the person who first had the idea for the
gathering. He exclaimed, "Let God be praised that he raised up
such a man!"

President Theodore Woolsey of Yale, one of Mary Dwight's descendants, gave the chief address, in which he stressed that Sarah had been for Jonathan "the resting-place of his soul." President Woolsey went on to point out that "the race, let me say here, has been rich in women 'whose works have praised them in the gates.' . . . This mother of us all, friends and kindred, deserves to be held in grateful remembrance."

The theme of the remarkable women in the clan was picked up again by John Todd, of Pittsfield, who confided, to the glee of the assembly, "I married a wife and it was years before I found out what made her so much my superior, but when I discovered that she belonged to the Edwards family and that she had their blood in her veins, I gave up the contest and have admitted all that she demanded ever since."

To track down so many offshoots of an intricately inter-married family, and then to arrange for their get-together had been a massive task. "It was difficult to find one to engineer the enterprise," reported the founding committee which had first discussed the idea. David Dudley Field, who had a princely summer place in Stockbridge, offered to put on a reception for everybody, and members of the church in Stockbridge volunteered to entertain the visitors in their homes. These invitations swung the meeting to the Berkshire Hills, though at first "most who were consulted were in favor of North-ampton." The current local minister, who happened to be a Hooker related to Sarah, said that the people of the town "have a feeling that they had the privilege of 'entertaining angels unawares' " when the Edwardses lived in Stockbridge.

Mrs. Sarah Edwards Tyler Henshaw from Illinois read an ode to their ancestors which included a section dedicated to "Sweet Sarah Pierrepont." It said, in part:

> For though thou might'st not all approve
> Thy children of today,
> Thy warnings would be filled with love;
> And sunlight, as from heaven above,
> Around thy words would play.

Dr. I. N. Tarbox gave an unintentionally humorous report on the old homestead in East Windsor, Connecticut.

> This house is now occupied by one of our adopted fellow-citizens from old Ireland by the name of Mr. Christopher McNary. . . . He is not well read up in the Edwardean history. . . . I am sorry to say he finds his chief occupation in raising tobacco.

Timothy's child, Mrs. Mary Edwards Whiting, the only living grandchild of the original family, was unable to come because she was then ninety-two, but she sent this message: "She wishes to bear her testimony at that meeting to God's covenant faithfulness and to his covenant mercies to her and hers." This idea recurred through the speeches of the two reunion days—here was a family that felt itself to have been touched by the purposes of Almighty God himself and sustained by him through all their generations. Prof. Edwards A. Park, of Andover Seminary, struck the most telling line of the assembly, though he apologized as he started to speak, explaining, "I have but recently left the Atlantic steamboat . . . and cannot uniformly believe myself to be on the land." Despite feeling wobbly, Dr. Park hit upon a central idea for the meeting when he said, "A family is a kind of Gulf Stream." That is what the Edwards family has actually been in American society.

One study in the New York Genealogical and Biographical Society asserts:

> Probably no two people married since the beginning of the 18th century have been the progenitors of so many distinguished persons as were Jonathan Edwards and Sarah Pierrepont.

One feature of the family that bedevils the genealogist, is "the large number of descendants who married first and second cousins." This returns us to an observation made in Chapter IV about the quality of intensity within the life of the Edwards house. People who were the products of that highly charged, affectionate, self-sufficient atmosphere felt that the only other persons who could truly understand them were those who had been shaped by the same sort of upbringing. They found they could explain themselves to cousins better than to other people. These intermarriages did not lead to degeneration of the blood line, but seemed to intensify the strengths. One result was the recurrence, through many generations, of women of black-eyed, oval-faced beauty, uncannily like Sarah.

Another family trait that the reunion exposed was that the Edwardses had been attracted to marry people of exceptional ability. One offspring married into the Sedgwick clan of Massachusetts. Another joined a Mather, thus doubling the ingredient of divinity in the bloodstream. Pierpont's daughter, Henrietta, married Eli Whitney. Timothy's oldest girl married Capt. Daniel Tyler, a Connecticut business tycoon whose "very large house . . . was long the wonder and admiration of the county."

Sarah Edwards Tyler, her granddaughter reminisced, was

> of a very dark complexion, with piercing black eyes that could read one's inmost soul. She was a woman of superior talents, wrote an excellent letter, was an insatiable reader.

An offspring of this lady invented a turbine wheel. Another descendant married the church leader Williston Walker. (Dean Willard Sperry, of Harvard Divinity School, used to tell his incoming classes, in his orientation lecture, "The line on which we hang everything here is Williston Walker." This church historian had a profound effect on theological education.) One Edwards girl married into the distinguished Heermance family, which fed deans into Princeton. Another married Daniel Gilman, president of Johns Hopkins and of the University of California. Edith Kermit Carow married Theodore Roosevelt. Kenaston Twitchell, himself heir to an outstanding banking family in New York, married the daughter of H. Alexander Smith, a New Jersey senator. (Twitchell took the part of Edwards in a pageant given in Stockbridge in 1936.) A recent Edwards married the sister of John Foster Dulles.

Another characteristic that streaked through the Edwards descendants was a pioneering opposition to slavery. When Jonathan, Jr., first saw whites and Negroes segregated at a Communion service, he wept and preached in 1791 a stinging sermon on *The Injustice and Impolicy of the Slave Trade.* The seven tall, intellectual sons of President Dwight "were foremost from the first among the anti-slavery men of the land" and were supported in their stands by the unusually talented, "cultivated . . . superior" women they each married.

And so the Gulf Stream of the family flowed across American culture, providing college presidents galore, headmasters of prep schools, theologians, poets, linguists, musicians, publishers, and one spunky woman who "was one of the few Democrats in the rock-ribbed Republican Township of Lisle, N.Y." How did all this energy flow out into society? Let us look quickly at what happened to the Edwards children who were left after the sad events of 1758.

On *Timothy* as the oldest son crashed down all the responsibility as head of the family. Though he was just twenty years old himself, he was forced to be in charge of five sisters and brothers, plus his niece and his defiant nephew. Timothy lived for a while near his bride's people in New Jersey, but moved back to Stockbridge to keep an eye on all the younger Edwardses. He hit upon the idea of becoming a merchant at a fortunate time, when "there was scarcely a store in the county." Prospering quickly, he had forty to fifty employees on his various farms and in stores when the American Revolution came along. He went to meet General Burgoyne and helped him at one critical point by giving him "lawful money" in return for the paper money ("of slight value") the general had been carrying. He also sold the government fifty tons of flour for worthless paper money. These patriotic gestures depleted his fortune, though he had fortunately invested in a land company over near what is now Binghamton, New York. Appointed one of the commissioners to settle the boundary line between Massachusetts and New York, he had seen the potentialities of the unopened country beyond the boundary. On his errands for the commission, he took along a son, Edward Edwards, who was six feet three inches tall, and so good-looking that the Indians gave him a name which meant "the handsome man." This son decided to settle in New York state in 1795, prospering in lumber enterprises in Broome County.

He was followed west by his brother Richard, a "brilliant lawyer" who settled in Cooperstown. Their sister Phebe was another distinct individual. Married to the treasurer of Andover Seminary, she was a woman so alert that when she was seventy-nine she took up reading about astronomy and was seen one cold winter evening happily hopping about in the snow, looking at the rings of Saturn through a telescope.

Another of Timothy's sons was William, who by the age of ten was handling heavy oxen, helping his father with the plowing, and when he was only twenty had set himself up in business as a tanner. He developed a process that reduced the cost while improving the volume and quality of making leather, thus changing the leather industry of the nation substantially. He in turn raised one son who organized the Dime Savings Bank in Brooklyn, another who was a wealthy silk importer, and a daughter who married a seminary president. All were active in philanthropy and church leadership.

Timothy's daughter, Rhoda, complicated the family tree by marrying a Northampton Dwight and having fifteen children. She had Sarah's stunning looks, and was "a wonder and joy to all who knew her, for intellectual power and brightness." Of Timothy's youngest child, the lady who sent greetings to the 1874 reunion, it was said that in her nineties her "mind was as clear as it was in the prime of life." In such a torrent of talent it is almost an artistic relief to come upon one grandson who was a pioneer hippie, went to sea and died, unmarried, in Acapulco.

*Mary Edwards Dwight* had a strange story. When the American Revolution began, Timothy Dwight refused to take arms against the king because in becoming a judge he had taken an oath of loyalty to the Crown. His life as a Tory became insupportable in Northampton, so he decided to try a crazy venture. He owned a twenty-mile-square tract of land near Natchez, Mississippi, and in May, 1776, he sailed off to New Orleans, taking two of the boys, leaving Mary, pregnant, with eight small children. He died of a strange germ in that new land, in 1777. The sons had a ghastly ordeal, trying to get back home. They were chased by Spaniards, robbed of their horses, lost their compass, had to cook turtles in order to eat, and flailed around in forests for five months. They finally stumbled out at Savannah "almost naked and perfectly Indianized." Dwight left a large estate, but many people owed him money, so his oldest son, Timothy, returned to Northampton to help straighten out his mother's business affairs. (Fortunately, Mary also had to help her a slave woman named Lil who "ruled the children of the house and indeed the whole street," according to town gossip.) Young Timothy Dwight had exhausted his eyes at Yale by too much reading in addition to a silly diet he had tried as an experiment. He returned to the farm, built himself up with outdoor work and careful diet, enhanced by a bottle of Madeira wine taken daily. So he was able to help Mary through the first years of crisis.

Then he went on to a parish at Greenfield Hill, Connecticut, where he had a variation on the quarrel his grandfather had once had. When Dwight was invited to be president of Yale, the parish voted to refuse to dismiss him. Their case was "there hath been a constant uninterrupted harmony and good agreement with the people of this place." Finally, the local Congregational ruling body had to step in and decided that the parish had to relinquish their pastor.

Dwight gave Yale an exhilarating administration, and managed also to dart off on such projects as his proposal in 1815— *Arguments for an American Bible Society and Objections to it Considered.* He had a yellow dog, Lion, a stray he had adopted after it had saved him when he was lost in a snowstorm. Lion always went to church when Dwight preached, lying sedately by the pulpit until the word "Amen" was pronounced. At that signal, Lion would get up and majestically head for the door.

It was Timothy Dwight who said that famous sentence which has been variously misquoted and attributed to others: "All that I am and all that I shall be, I owe to my mother." Like his grandfather, he was a man of brilliance and conflict. "Adored" by Yale undergraduates, scorned by some of his colleagues, he unquestionably changed the history of his time.

Mary's other children were colorfully assorted. Sereno, who had been with his father on that horrible trip in Mississippi, became a surgeon. Theodore became editor of the *Hartford Courant.* Nathanial was a doctor who sparked the establishment of the first hospital for mental diseases in Connecticut. His interest in psychiatry came because one of his brothers, Erastus, was unhinged after he was shot at during the Tory unpleasantness. Erastus lived on as a recluse in Northampton, slipping over at night to his brother Cecil's house, to take a solitary meal from a table that was always left set for him after the family went to bed. (Cecil was a sheriff and member of the Massachusetts General Court.) Elizabeth Dwight married a rich banker and their son, Theodore Woolsey, became president of Yale, and a trusted adviser to President Rutherford B. Hayes. He recalled that his mother had the black-eyed charm that marked many of Sarah's descendants, and was "highly intelligent and thoughtful . . . a great reader."

Lucy, who had been the valiant helper of Esther and Sarah, continued to be the family rock. She took over the Burr children until Timothy was able to relieve her in 1759. After living first with the Parsons, and then with Timothy, Lucy was married in 1764 to Jahleel Woodbridge, a man two years younger than she, who was nephew of the pioneer Stockbridge schoolmaster. Jahleel, a Princeton graduate, was a close friend of Timothy Edwards. He became a state senator and judge, and was highly respected, except for the rowdy interlude of Shay's Rebellion when a gang of hoodlums broke in on the Woodbridge house because the owner was considered "silk stocking aristocracy." Lucy had a flock of children, including a daughter who married a son of Timothy's. At the 1874 reunion, Joseph E. Woodbridge, of Brooklyn, recalled how his grandfather Jahleel would ask him to read a passage from Deuteronomy about the religious instruction of children: "And ye shall teach them your children, speaking of them when thou sittest in thine house." The self-giving Lucy found a husband worthy of her and built a home where faith was alive in daily practice. Her children's descendants leaned to medicine and politics. One was controller of the United States Treasury and another was a strong congressman from Ohio. Edwards would have rejoiced to see that Lucy's house was "a little church," as he had once said a house ideally should be.

*Jonathan, Jr.*, had been fascinated by Indians ever since he had played with his Stockbridge neighbors. He had also trailed after Gideon Hawley, eagerly asking him questions. As a result, he became a philologist and published in 1788 a study, *Observations on the Language of the Muhekaneew (Mohawk) Indians* in which he pointed out the similarities between Hebrew and the Mohawk tongue. In the Princeton archives is an engaging letter he wrote in June, 1768, to his older brother, Timothy. Jonathan inquired warmly for Timothy's health, and that of Sally Burr and "Mr. Pollock," a swain of his sister Eunice's. Then, in the way of all boys away at school, Jonathan, Jr., slyly slipped in a remark about how he could use some more shirts and shoes.

Jonathan stayed on at Princeton as a tutor during an unsettled period when the college lost two successors to Edwards in rapid succession. Then Jonathan was one of the greeters lined up to meet John Witherspoon when that Scotsman arrived to give Princeton, at last, a long and sturdy leadership. Jonathan became minister of Third Church in New Haven, a group of people who had split off from Second Church in 1767. Like his father, he had a stormy time with churches. His flinty integrity shows in the title of an ordination sermon he preached for the minister in the New Hartford, Connecticut, church. It was *The Duty of the Minister of the Gospel to Preach the Truth.* Like his father, this son had a character that combined theological steel with a capacity for tenderness. He continued to be devoted to his family, and when Timothy Dwight was married in 1777, Jonathan performed the ceremony. It was held in Pierpont's house, an indication that the clan continued to cherish one another, though the mother who had first bound them in affectionate ties was gone.

Also like his father, this namesake finally came out in a role as a college president—at Union College in Schenectady, New York. He continued to be intrigued by Indian studies all his life, and when Ezra Stiles had to entertain some Mississippi Indians in 1793, he turned to Jonathan, Jr., to help him talk to them. This son died at fifty-six, living only a year or so longer than his father, and like his father had preached on the first Sunday of the year he died on the eerie text: "This year thou shalt die."

*Sarah Edwards Parsons,* the oldest daughter in the family, had a less conspicuous life than the others. She and Elihu moved to Goshen, Connecticut, where he turned more to farming than to law. Decent, undistinguished, they raised eleven children. Her great-grandson became a senator and a governor of New York State. His sister married Seth Merrill Gates, an early abolitionist who was twice a member of Congress. Another of her great-grandsons was William Ketchum, a mayor of Buffalo.

*Susanna* married Eleazar Porter when she was twenty-one. She was his second wife, and he became a judge of Probate Court. The family clannishness showed up again in her son, who married Fidelia Dwight. His son, Timothy Dwight Porter, owned a large estate, and from this line came Quincy Porter, the late professor of music and master of Pierson College at Yale. Porter's father and grandfather had also taught at Yale, where President Kingman Brewster said of him: "Quincy Porter was one of those rare and wonderful people; a genuinely free spirit. He helped to liberate the rest of us from self-consciousness and conformity." So a certain individuality and courage is discernible in the family blood line till this day.

Eunice was still small when she lost her parents, so she did not have as many years of that influence on her character. She was pretty enough to snag an eminently eligible husband, Thomas Pollock, son of the governor of North Carolina, the "wealthiest man in the state." (That was a solid family, descended from John Warham who had come from Exeter, England, in 1630 and organized the first Presbyterian church in this country.) After Pollock died, Eunice married Robert Hunt of New Jersey. She had a son, George, who lived in Philadelphia and was a crony of his cousin, Aaron Burr. Her comparatively bland career may document the theory that the quality of Sarah's training had a good deal to do with the way the children turned out.

Pierpont was only eight when he lost his mother and had to go to live in Timothy's crowded household. Bewildered by all the sudden changes in his life, he ran away once and grew up rather haphazardly. He kept the spelling of the name that is in the Edwards family Bible, a gift from "Benjamin Pierpont" in 1728. He is listed under that spelling in the Princeton college roster for 1768. Bright, mischievous, and sprightly, he became a judge of the U.S. District Court, and one of the group of able young men who dominated Connecticut politics in the 1790's. (They called themselves "The Nocturnal Society of Stelligeri.") His son became a United States senator and governor of his state. But Pierpont, like Eunice, demonstrated that natural talent and charm needed character training.

The sequel to Esther's story is national folklore, because of her son, Aaron Burr. Sally Burr, in spite of her "crooked neck," achieved a fine husband, Tapping Reeve, who came as a young Princeton graduate to be tutor to the Burr children and ended by marrying his charge, Sally. They lived in a handsome house in Litchfield, Connecticut, where Reeve started the first law school in America, and one of its pupils was Horace Mann. Reeve became the chief justice of the state Supreme Court, and this worthy couple were always baffled by Sally's brother.

When he was four years old, little Aaron ran away for three days from the distracted Timothy Edwards, who was too young for the large burdens that had piled upon him, and, as Burr recalled, he "licked me like a sack." When he was seven, the defiant small boy pelted a stylish lady with ripe cherries. He finally managed to graduate from Princeton in 1772, then tried unenthusiastically to study theology with Bellamy. After nine months of that, he announced to his grandfather's crony that "the road to heaven was open to all alike," and proceeded to gallop off on a borrowed horse. (Uncle Timothy had to pay for the horse.) Burr then tried to join the army, chasing a regiment for twenty-eight miles to catch up with them. A servant was sent by Timothy to try to stop him. "How do you expect to take me back?" Aaron defied him, and bit off his umbilical cord forever.

Burr had the fatal gift of easy charm. Esther had it too, but she had parents who saw that her charm was bounded by discipline. Her son inherited her facile charisma, without the character that saved Esther from slickness. As our friend, the eugenicist A. E. Winship says: "The right training would have enabled Aaron Burr to go into history as the noblest Roman of them all."

This strand of the family line dwindled out when Burr's daughter, Theodosia, wife of Joseph Alston, governor of South Carolina, was lost at sea in 1812. The specter of Burr always hovered over the Edwards family, and one of Timothy's sons named his boy Alexander Hamilton Edwards, as one effort to make up for the tragic trail left by the family enigma.

The frail *Elizabeth*, without her mother, wilted and died at fourteen. So just one question remains about this family tree— What children might have resulted from the marriage of two people so extraordinary as *Jerusha* and David Brainerd?

At the family reunion in 1874, Dr. William B. Sprague, of Albany, said that when Sereno Dwight* was gathering material for his book about his great-grandfather, he interviewed a very old man, Dr. Lathrop, of West Springfield. Lathrop told of hearing Edwards preside at family prayers, and commented that "he never heard another prayer that brought heaven and earth so near together."

The first event in the lives of all the children was when their father wrote down the date of their birth in the Bible. That Bible had been a wedding gift, and it was the core of the Edwardses' life together. Every life within that house was entrusted, from its first hour, to the care of the One who was, they were confident, the Living God. As a result their household was one in which heaven and earth were near together.

When Edwards choked out his last words, he spoke accurately as he had always tried to do. It was truly "an uncommon union."

---

* He was chaplain of the United States Senate and president of Hamilton College.

# Sources

Many individuals have helped me in this pursuit of Edwards as lover and father. Among them are: J. Walter Edwards, Bridgehampton, N.Y.; Howard Tracy, Waterbury, Conn.; Mrs. J. Douglas Brown, Princeton, N.J.; Dr. Morgan P. Noyes, Montclair, N.J.; Miss Grace Pierpont Fuller, Woodbridge, Conn.

The following agencies have courteously allowed me to delve in their files: The Congregational Library, Boston, Mass.; The New Jersey Historical Society, Newark, N.J.; The New York Genealogical and Biographical Society; The New Haven Historical Society; The Northampton Historical Society; The Princeton University Library; The Union Theological Seminary Library.

Robert Lowell confided his difficulties with Edwards as subject in the 1958 Paris Review Symposium *Writers at Work.* A letter on January 30, 1960, from Miss Grace Pierpont Fuller enhances my suspicion that there has been a simple matter of personal taste in the discrepancy in the spelling of Pierpont v. Pierrepont. She wrote: "My ancestor was Joseph the 2nd (?) son. . . . That first Joseph moved to the North Haven section of New Haven and was a farmer. The youngest son went to New York and was the ancestor of all the swells, including those who incline to spell it Pierrepont."

CHAPTER I. JONATHAN EDWARDS MEETS HIS MATCH

The first quotation is from *Teilhard de Chardin: A Biographical Study*, by Claude Cuénot, tr. by Vincent Colimore; ed. by René Hague (Helicon Press, Inc., 1966). *The Life and Character of the Late Reverend . . . Mr. Jonathan Edwards*, by Samuel Hopkins (published in Boston in 1765), is the fundamental memoir, reprinted many times. I have used the version in Sereno Edwards Dwight's *The Works of President Edwards with a Memoir of His Life* (London: Ball & Arnold, 1840).

Other background sources
Adams, James T., *History of American Life*. The Macmillan Company, 1927.
Allen, A. V. G., *Jonathan Edwards*. Houghton Mifflin Company, 1890.
Beals, Carleton, *Our Yankee Heritage*. David McKay Company, Inc., 1955.
Carroll, Peter N., *Puritanism and the Wilderness*. Columbia University Press, 1969.
Gipson, Lawrence H., *The Northern Plantations* (Vol. 2 of *The British Empire Before the American Revolution*). London: Caxton Press, 1936.
Laurence, Henry, *The Not Quite Puritans*. Little, Brown and Company, 1928.
Marlowe, George F., *Churches of Old New England*. The Macmillan Company, 1947.
Miller, Perry, *Jonathan Edwards* (American Men of Letters Series). William Sloane, Associates, Inc., 1949.
——— *The New England Mind*, 2 vols. Harvard University Press, 1953 and 1954.
——— *Errand Into the Wilderness*. Belknap Press Book (Harvard University Press), 1956.
Moffat, R. B., *Pierrepont Genealogy from Norman Times to 1913*, Vol. I. 1913.

Morgan, Edmund S., *The Gentle Puritan*. Yale University Press, 1962.

Morison, Samuel E., *Intellectual Life of Colonial New England*. New York University Press, 1956.

Winslow, Ola Elizabeth, *Jonathan Edwards, 1703–1758*. The Macmillan Company, 1940.

*Pamphlets*

Ahlstrom, Sydney, "The Saybrook Platform," *Bulletin of the Congregational Library*, October, 1959, and January, 1960.

"New Haven Old and New," a scrapbook compiled by the New Haven Historical Society.

## CHAPTER II. A CHECKERED COURTSHIP

Edwards' *Journal* is ubiquitous. I have consulted both Vergilius Ferm (ed.), *Puritan Sage* (Library Publishers, Inc., 1953), and David Levin (ed.), *Jonathan Edwards* (Hill & Wang, Inc., 1969).

*Other background sources*

Morris, William S., "The Young Jonathan Edwards." Unpublished doctoral thesis, The University of Chicago, 1955.

Northend, Mary, *Colonial Homes and Their Furnishings*. Little, Brown and Company, 1912.

Shea, Daniel B., Jr., *Spiritual Autobiography in Early America*. Princeton University Press, 1968.

Walker, Williston, *The Creeds and Platforms of Congregationalism*. Charles Scribner's Sons, 1893.

## CHAPTER III. "YES, YOURS, MY LOVE, IS THE RIGHT HUMAN FACE"

The chapter title is a line by Edwin Muir from his poem of the same name, in *Collected Poems*, 2d ed. (London: Oxford University Press, 1965). The most useful resource for this chapter was a collection of loose clippings, letters, and memorabilia at the Northampton Historical Society.

*Other background sources*
Allis, Marguerite, *The Connecticut River*. G. P. Putnam's Sons, 1939.
Bowen, Catherine Drinker, *John Adams and the American Revolution*. Little, Brown and Company, 1949.
Earle, Alice M., *Customs and Fashions in Old New England*. Charles Scribner's Sons, 1893.
Johnson, Clifton, *Historic Hampshire*. Milton Bradley Company, 1932.
Lyman, C., *Northampton in the Days of Jonathan Edwards*. Metcalf Company, undated.
Trumbull, Russell, *History of Northampton*, Vols. I and II. Norton, 1898.
"Early Northampton," *Bulletin of the Betty Allen Chapter, D.A.R.*, 1914.
"First Parish Historical Sketch." Gazette Company, 1878.

CHAPTER IV. "HEAVEN IS A WORLD OF LOVE"

The opening quotation by Erik H. Erikson from "Reflections on Womanhood," is reprinted by permission from *Daedalus, Journal of the American Academy of Arts and Sciences* (Boston, Mass.), Vol. 93, No. 2.

*Background sources*
Bacon, David, *Memoirs of Eminently Pious Women*. Daniel McLeod Company, 1833.
Crawford, M., *Social Life in Old New England*. Little, Brown and Company, 1915.
Kelly, J., *Early Domestic Architecture of New England*. Yale University Press, 1924.
Stiles, Dan (pseud.), *The Town of Woodbury*. Sugar Ball Press, undated.

Todd, John, *Lectures to Children.* J. H. Butler, 1834.

Tucker, Louis Leonard, *Puritan Protagonist.* University of North Carolina Press, 1962.

Winship, A. E., *Jukes-Edwards.* R. L. Myers & Company, 1900.

Woodward, William E., *The Way Our People Lived.* E. P. Dutton & Co., Inc., 1944.

*Pamphlets*

Clark, I. W., "A Wifely Estimate of Edwards," *Christian World*, Oct. 3, 1903.

de Normandie, James, "Jonathan Edwards at Portsmouth, New Hampshire," *Proceedings of the Massachusetts Historical Society*, 1902.

## CHAPTER V. THE ACTIVE LATCHSTRING

Blake, Francis, *History of Princeton, Massachusetts*, Vols. I and II. Printed by the town, 1915.

Dunbar, Seymour, *History of Travel in America.* Tudor Publishing Company, 1937.

Earle, Alice M., *Stagecoach and Tavern Days.* The Macmillan Company, 1905.

Grosart, Alexander (ed.), *Selections from the Unpublished Writings of Jonathan Edwards.* Edinburgh, 1865.

Levin, David, *The Puritan in the Enlightenment.* Rand McNally & Company, 1963.

Montgomery, Louisa, *Pioneer Homemaker.* Privately printed, 1903.

Paterson, William, *Glimpses of Colonial Society.* J. B. Lippincott Company, 1933.

*Pamphlets*

Manning, Harold, "Invention and Discovery," *Journal of the Patent Office Society*, March, 1950.

Williams, Stanley, "Six Letters of Jonathan Edwards to Joseph Bellamy," *The New England Quarterly*, Vol. I, 1928.

### Chapter VI. What Was Driving Him?

Edwards, Jonathan, *Religious Affections*, ed. by John E. Smith. Yale University Press, 1959.
—— *Freedom of the Will*, ed. by Paul Ramsey. Yale University Press, 1957.
McGiffert, A. C., *Jonathan Edwards*. Harper & Brothers, 1932.
Parkes, H. B., *The Fiery Puritan*. Minton, Balch & Company, 1930.
Turnbull, Ralph G., *Jonathan Edwards, the Preacher*. Baker Book House, 1958.
Van Every, Dale, *Forth to the Wilderness*. William Morrow & Company, Inc., 1961.
Wertenbaker, Thomas J., *The Golden Age of Colonial Culture*. New York University Press, undated; Cornell University Press, 1959.


*Pamphlets*
Brown, Charles, "Jonathan Edwards in 1958," *Ministers' Quarterly*, 1958.
Worthy, Harold F., "Pilgrim Church Records," *Bulletin of the Congregational Library*, October, 1961.


### Chapter VII. The Awakening: A Dubious Blessing

The fragment by Robert Lowell is from "After the Surprising Conversions," in *Lord Weary's Castle* (Harcourt, Brace & Company, Inc., 1946). Used by permission of Harcourt, Brace, Jovanovich, Inc. The letter from J. Walter Edwards was written on November 22, 1962.


*Other background sources*
Boswell, James, *The Life of Samuel Johnson*. E. P. Dutton & Company, Inc., 1931.

Edwards, Jonathan, *Thoughts on the Revivals of Religion in Northampton*. S. Butler Company, 1819.

Henry, Stuart C., *George Whitfield: Wayfaring Witness*. Abingdon Press, 1957.

Hitt, Russell T. (ed.), *Heroic Colonial Christians.* J. B. Lippincott Company, 1966.

Klein, M. M., "The American Whig, William Livingston of New York." Unpublished doctoral thesis, Columbia University, 1954.

Trinterud, Leonard J., *The Forming of an American Tradition*. The Westminster Press, 1959.

## CHAPTER VIII. TO THE BREAKING POINT AND BACK

The lines by Dan Sullivan appeared in *Commonweal*, July 22, 1966, and are reprinted with the permission of Commonweal Publishing Company, Inc.

*Background sources*

James, William, *The Varieties of Religious Experience*. It was printed first in 1902. I have used the Modern Library edition.

Schlesinger, Elizabeth B., "The Philosopher's Wife and the Wolf at the Door," *American Heritage*, August, 1957.

## CHAPTER IX. RUMBLINGS

*Genealogy of the Hon. Edwards Pierpont*, folio in the New York Genealogical Society.

Grant, Leonard, "A Preface to Jonathan Edwards' Financial Difficulties," *Journal of Presbyterian History*, March, 1967.

## CHAPTER X. TIME OUT FOR TWO MORE ROMANCES

Emerson, Joseph, *Diary, August 1, 1748 to April 9, 1749*. John Wilson and Sons, 1911.

Edwards, Jonathan, *The Life of the Rev. David Brainerd*. London: Burton & Smith, 1818.

Gilchrist, Beth, *The Life of Mary Lyon*. Houghton Mifflin Company, 1910.

Howard, Philip (ed.), *The Life and Diary of David Brainerd*. The Moody Press, 1949.

Kendall, Benjamin, *The Ipswich Emersons*. David Clapp & Company, 1900.

Tuttle, Walter, *Colonial Holidays*. Doubleday & Company, Inc., 1910.

*Colonial Families of America*, Vol. 4. National Americana Society, 1930.

CHAPTER XI. PRESENT: TENSE

Faust, Clarence H., and Johnson, Thomas H. (eds.), *Jonathan Edwards, Representative Selections*. American Book Company, 1935.

Wright, Andrew, *The Life and Character of the Late Rev. Learned and pious Jonathan Edwards*. Privately printed, 1804.

CHAPTER XII. A SEASON OF HARVEST AND RESPITE

The opening quotation from *The Fellowship of the Ring*, by J. R. R. Tolkien, is used with the permission of Houghton Mifflin Company.

Background sources

Hawley, Gideon, *Book of Journal After My Mission into the Country [of] Six Nations*. Original Manuscript in Congregational Library, Boston.

Grant, Anne, *Memoirs of an American Lady*. The Macmillan Company, 1902.

Peattie, Roderick (ed.), *The Berkshires*. Vanguard Press, Inc., 1948.

Sloane, Eric, *American Yesterdays*. Funk & Wagnalls Company, 1956.

*The Berkshire Hills* (American Guide Series). Funk & Wagnalls Company, 1956.

## CHAPTER XIII. TWO PRESIDENCIES AT PRINCETON

The poem "Colonel B." is reprinted with the permission of *The New Yorker*. The Burr letters are in the General Manuscript Collection at Princeton University.

*Other background sources*
Boyer, Charles S., *Old Inns and Taverns in West Jersey*. Camden County Historical Society, 1962.

Cawley, James S., and Margaret, *Along the Old York Road*. Rutgers University Press, 1965.

Collins, V. L., *President Witherspoon: A Bibliography*, Vol. 1. Princeton University Press.

Hall, V. L., *History of the Presbyterian Church in Trenton*, Anson Randolph Company, 1859.

Lane, Wheaton Joshua, *From Indian Trail to Iron Horse* (Vol. I of *Princeton History of New Jersey*). Princeton University Press, 1939.

McCormick, Richard P., *New Jersey from Colony to State*. D. Van Nostrand Company, Inc., 1964.

Stearns, J. F., *History of First Church, Newark*. *Daily Advertiser*, 1853.

Van Sickle, Emogene, *The Old York Road*. Privately printed, 1936.

Walker, George, *Princeton Sketches*. G. P. Putnam's Sons, 1893.

Wertenbaker, Thomas J., *Princeton, 1746–1896*. Princeton University Press, 1939.

*Miscellaneous sources*
Edwards, Jonathan, "True Grace as Distinguished . . ." etc. Shepard Kollock, 1791.

Lunny, Robert, *Early Maps of North America*. New Jersey
Historical Society, 1961.

*New Jersey Road Maps of the 18th Century*. Princeton University Library, 1964.

*Iconography of New Jersey*, Vols. 5 and 6. New Jersey Historical
Society.

Ogden, Aaron, *Autobiography*. New Jersey Historical Society,
undated.

*Memorial Book of the Sesquicentennial Celebration, 1898*.
Princeton.

Olson, Alison, "The Founding of Princeton University," *New
Jersey History*, Autumn, 1969.

*Records of the Town of Newark, 1666–1836*. New Jersey Historical Society, 1864.

*Proceedings of the New Jersey Historical Society, 1965–1966*,
Vol. X, pp. 170–172, and Vol. III, No. 2.

Nelson, William, "Discovery and Early History of New Jersey."
Passaic County Historical Society, June 11, 1872.

Rice, Howard C., "Jonathan Edwards at Princeton," *Chronicle
of the Princeton University Library*, SV No. 2, Winter, 1954.

CHAPTER XIV. "A FAMILY IS A KIND OF GULF STREAM"

*Memorial Volume of the Edwards Family Meeting*. Congregational Publishing Society, 1874.

Dwight, Benjamin, *History of the Descendants of John Dwight*.
John Two & Son, 1874.

Edwards, William, *Timothy and Rhoda Ogden Edwards*. Robert
Clark Company, 1903.

Smith, E. Y., *Descendants of William Edwards*. New York
Genealogical and Biographical Society, undated.

Twitchell, Mary, *The Edwards Family in Chenango County*.
Lisle, 1947.

Walker, O. B., *Lisle: State, Town, Village*. The Pennysaver
Company, 1937.

Dr. Brewster's remark was in *The New York Times*, November 11, 1966.